Education in North-East India

Education in North-East India

N B Biswas

SHIPRA

(2008 Reprint, First published in 1999)

Rs. 895, US$ 30

ISBN: 978-81-7541-409-9

2013 Impression

Education in North-East India

Published by:

SHIPRA PUBLICATIONS
LG 18-19, Pankaj Central Market,
I.P. Ext., Patparganj, Delhi 110092
Ph.: 91 11 22235152/6152; 9650028065
info@shiprapublication.com
www.shiprapublication.com

FOREWORD

The formal or institutional education has a colonial origin in most parts of North East India, in the sense that the educational institutions started in this region during the British colonial rule. In the two valleys of Assam-the Brahmaputra and the Barak, and in the plains of Tripura and Manipur, the tols and moktabs or similar traditional insitutions imparted learning to a very small section of the population in pre-colonial period. In these areas also the mass education made a beginning in the colonial period, although the British educational policy in India had a very limited objective of creating a lettered manpower to serve administration in the subordinate cadres. In the hill areas, the pioneers of progress in the field of education were, however, the western missionaries who, along with reading and writing, emphasised training in useful art and crafts. The proselytisation was, no doubt, their main objective. Nevertheless, the most significant contribution of these missioneries was that they converted the tribal dialects into written languages and prepared the primers for the schools. In this backgound, the progress of education in the hill areas of north-east in a short period since 19th century must be considered as spectacular by any standard. The development was more rapid in the post-indepdence period. There are now about five hundred colleges, including a few for legal, medical, technical, and teacher education, and nine Universities for the general education and two agricultural Universities. Needless to say that the primary, secondary and higher secondary schools are proportionate to the number of instititions for higher education. The literacy rate in the region is also comparable with national average. Mizoram has attained the glory of the second highest literacy rate in the country, although the first high school in Aizawl was established only in 1944. Arunachal Pradesh the land of rising sun or where sun rises first in India, was the latest among the seven sister states of North East India to be ruled by the British. The beginning of modern education in Arunachal was virtually after India's independence. The Towang monastery had been imparting education since ancient time, but it was by and large limited to theosophical learning. The western missionaries entered the field in British time, but the progress till 1947 was not very significant. However, in fifty years since independence the state has reached the highest stage of education with at least seven degree colleges, one University and a regional institute of science and technology. The state government is the main agency for promotion of education in Arunachal Pradesh, but the socio-cultural organisations like the Ramakrishna Mission and the Dony-Polo Mission are also doing excellent works in the state. A Ramakrishna Mission School in Purushattamnagar is now one of the best schools in our country. Similarly, the schools managed by the Dony-Polo Mission in Pasighat and other places are rooted in the culture of the Arunachalis. It must be appreciated that despite geographical isolation and infrastructural and economic backwardness, education is one area in which the north-eastern region of India could make rapid strides towards progress in the post-independence period.

The development of education is an important area of research interest of our scholars. Besides reconstructing a complete profile of educational history, it is important to understand the extent to which education has been able to integrate the culture of the people into the contents and philosophy of learning and the nature of impact that education has been able to make on the socio-economic and cultural advance of the people. My colleague, Dr N B Biswas has made a serious attempt in this direction in his EDUCATION IN NORTH EASTERN INDIA. A Reader in Education, Assam University, Silchar, Dr Biswas had earlier worked in Arunachal University. He utilised his stay in Arunachal in studying the role of education in the development of the people of Arunachal Pradesh in anthropological and historical perspectives. Therefore, his present study deals with the development of education in north-eastern region of India with special reference to Arunachal Pradesh. It covers a broad range of themes in education, and it is based on both primary and secondary data, including the personal experience of the author in the field. I am sure that the book will be appreciated by those for whom it is written. Nevertheless, there is no last word in research and a pioneering work is always improved upon between the editions. My colleague will welcome academic comments and suggestions for the next edition.

J B Bhattacharjee

education in the development of the people of Arunachal Pradesh in anthropological and historical perspectives. Therefore, the present study deals with the development of education in a particular region of India with special reference to Arunachal Pradesh. It covers a broad range of themes in education, and it is based on both primary and secondary data including the personal experience of the author in the field. I am sure, that the book will be appreciated by those for whom it is written. Nevertheless, there is no last word in research and a pioneering work is always improved upon between the editions. My colleague will welcome academic comments and suggestions for the next edition.

J. B. Bhattacharjee

PREFACE

The present book-the first of its kind-encompasses the entire domain of education in North-Eastern Indian with special reference to Arunachal Pradesh. This volume is an outcome of my long reserarch experience and intimate contact with the tribal people inhabiting different parts of the region. Educators generally agree that education takes place in a specific socio-cultural context. But we are not always clear and precise about the myriad of ways in which cultural factors influence the process of schooling, teaching and learning. More often than not, our sensitivity to and the lack of knowledge regarding the role of tribal culture in education lead to unsound educational policies, ineffective educational practices, and unfair assessment of learners. Accordingly, the primary purpose of this book is to examine education and the development of the people of the state of Arunachal in anthropological and historical perspectives.

The work in a most comprehensive way wants to acquaint the readers within a brief span not only with the Modern Period of education in North East and Arunachal Pradesh but also of the ancient time the type of education which was practiced in the region. The book is the result of indepth study of various sources. Primary data were procured through field study with the help of set of structured tools. A vast variety of secondary sources particularly anthropological and historical research studies conducted by renowned anthropologist and historians like Verriar Elwin, L.N. Chakraborty, H.K Barpujari, J. B. Bhattacharjee, S.N. Sarma and also the sources such as central and state government documents, non-governmental publications, census reports, etc., proved useful for the analysis of the educational system in a national perspective. So far Arunachal is concerened nothing was known definitely about the conditions prevailing in the area prior to 18th century. We have practically no material written or unwritten, relating to education of this area other than some oral literature. Many writes from outside and within, have written books, pamphlets and articles on Arunachal and writings have been printed and published from time to time. But is is a matter of regret that none of the publications highlights any stage of education in Arunachal Pradesh such as what it was and how the present formal system of education came up.

In order to make the beginning in this process the present volume has been composed. The information of the book is emperical and provided with scientific methodology. The book begins with an interactive analysis of education and development in North East which is followed by a review of the major historical description of the development of education starting from monastic education which has come down to the area of Tawang from China and Tibet and the evolution of formal education in the state of Arunachal. Third chapter of the book presents a decade-wise development of school education (pre-primary, primary, secondary, higher secondary education) which is followed by a trend analysis. The remaining five chapters deal with Higher Education, Teacher Education, Adult and Non-formal, Vocational and Technical Education, Women Education and Educational Management. The last chapter presents the brief review of Panchayatiraj and Educational development in the region. The most vital function of education under planning is not merely imparting knowledge or skills, but developing attitudes and generating a "Climate of growth" and so educational researchers and training have assumed an importance and urgency inadequately appreciated.

Thus I hope this book will enable the students, researchers, teachers and planners to realise the gravity of the problems and prospects of education and the real needs of the region and of our tribal bretheren in Arunachal for formulation and implementation of education policy in the state. This book will be a great help to the students of education (Undergraduate, Postgraduate and at the research level) in North Eastern India in general and Arunachal in particular.

Efforts have been made to cover the various aspects of education in this book, suggestions for its improvement are, however, welcome.

I owe a great deal to my colleagues in Arunachal University and Assam University, Education Experts, Officers, Teachers and Librarians of various institutions in North Eastern India, who extended their full co-operation and help during various stages of my research including finalisation of the book.

I would like to express my gratefulness and sincere gratitude to Prof J B Bhattacharjee, Vice Chancellor, Assam University for writing the foreword of the book.

Assam University, Silchar **N B Biswas**

CONTENTS

I

DEVELOPMENT OF EDUCATION

An Overview

Introduction

The North-Eastern region of the country comprises the states of Arunachal Pradesh, Assam, Manipur, Meghalaya, Mizoram, Nagaland and Tripura. All these units, excepting the two former princely states of Manipur and Tripura, constituted the erstwhile composite State of Assam. North-Eastern India has been historically subject to the penetration by the people of Mongolian origin and culture in the same way as the north-western passes of the Himalayas had provided for the entry of the Aryans. According to an account by a Naga social scientist : Successive hordes of people of Mongolian races from China and other parts of South-east Asia had passed to the arid mountains and fertile valleys which by the process of time came to be known as Burma, Meiteiland (Manipur), Kamrup (Assam), Tipperah, Bhutan, Sikkim... . Probably many of the earlier migrants passed on into Bengal and merged with the Dravidians and Aryans who were already there from the west and south. In course of time the two races mixed together through marriage, culture, exchange of ideas and values, the outcome of which was a new breed of people.

These Mongolian migrants, the Naga author goes on to say, afterwards known by different names, such as, Kirata, Cine, Koch,

Hajong, Dalo, Garo, Khasi, Mikir, Dimael, Arlung, Chintya, Moran, Kachari, Tipperah, Laling, Rabha, Mech, Lushai, Lakher, Pawi, Arakanese, Poi, Chakma, Kuki, Naga, Meitei, Adi (Abhor), Apatani, Mishmi (Mishing), Turung, Khamyan, etc., settled in the valleys (Brahmaputra, Surma, Manipur) as well as the mountains and the hills which rise from the plains of the Bay of Bengal near Chittagong, Cachar and Assam on one side and from Burma on the other.

However, all these tribes were not homogeneous, but a medley of different races, divided into numerous tribes, sub-tribes and clans under the Mongolian race, different in origin, distinct in language, diverse in physique, character, culture and society, depending upon the peripherial geographical locality. They were often, as we find them today, at loggerheads with one another and with outsiders as well, for which all of them had severely suffered in many ways. The most important of them is a certain lack of cohesion among the people of these origins, arising from the extreme heterogeneity of ethnic composition, further strengthened by the isolation of the different communities, in the north east, imposed by the difficult mountainous terrains.

The region covered 2,55,083 Square Kilometre which form only about 7.95% of the total area of India. There are 3,15,47,314 population in the region which constitute 3.5% of the total population of India. The region is sparsely populated with a density of population far below 100 per square kilometre with the exception of Assam and Tripura each of which has about the same density as the National figure of 273 per Sq. Km. The North - East states are predominantly inhabited by a large number of schedule tribes having different dialects/languages and cultural pattern. There are about ninety nine tribes in the region consists of 81,42,624 population and form 12.02% of the total tribal population in India (1991). Most of the states in the region are having more than 70% tribal population except Assam and Tripura.

The people of the region are having more than 60 dialects. The North-Eastern region is marked by under development, inaccessibility, isolation, low population density, and dispersed population, largely hilly and difficult terrain, low levels of

States	Area	Population	No. of tribes & sub tribes	Density	% of Total Population aged 0-6	Literacy Rate			SC/ST Population	No. of Districts 1991	No. of Villages 1984
						Total	Male	Fem.			
ARUNACHAL PRADESH	83743 Sqkm.	864558 M-465004 F-399554	22 110	10	21.12	41.59	51.45	29.69	SC-4052 ST-550351	11	3257
ASSAM	78438 " "	22414322 M-11657989 F-10756333	23	286	19.73	52.89	61.87	43.03	SC-1659412 ST-2874441	23	21995
MANIPUR	22327 " "	1837149 M-938359 F-897890	7 22	82	16.69	59.89	71.63	47.60	SC-37105 ST-632173	8	2035
MEGHALAYA	22429 " "	1774778 M-907687 F-867091	3	79	22.18	49.10	53.12	44.85	SC-9072 ST-1517927	5	4902
MIZORAM	21081 " "	689756 M-358978 F-330778	6	33	18.60	82.27	85.61	78.60	SC-691 ST-653565	3	721
NAGALAND	16579 " "	1209546 M-641282 F-568264	17	73	17.15	61.67	67.62	54.75	SC-NIL ST-1060822	7	1112
TRIPURA	10486 " "	2757205 M-1417930 F-1339275	19 17	262	18.03	60.44	70.58	49.65	SC-451116 ST-853345	3	856
INDIA	255083 " "	31547314 M-16387229 F-15160085	97	124	21.80				8142624 25.81%	60	34878

urbanisation, high cost of living and developing infrastructure and insurgency movements in certain parts. These distinctive features have implications for educational development as well. Although there are marked intra-regional differences, the region as a whole is far behind any other parts of the country in respect of several indicators of development including education.

Education and Development

Education interacts and is interdependent with the process of development. Social structures, policies and goals exert their influence on the education sector, as on other sectors, while the education sector influences economic and social development by inducing change in technology through the systematic application of scientific and other knowledge, in skill and specialized knowledge for specialized tasks as a consequence of their division and differentiation, and in values and attitude to provide the necessary incentives for increasing productive efficiency, The net change in growth is the result of the modern education, assisted by changes in values and attitudes. For various reasons, it has become an accepted practice to relate development of society to the quality and quantity of education it imparts. Thus, it has become impossible to talk of development without bringing in the subject of education. What should be understood by the word education? Following Robert F. Hutchins, we shall take it "to be deliberate, organized attempt to help people to become intelligent". The link between education and development then becomes obvious. An intelligent man no doubt will be more effective in any profession than an unintelligent one. Since education is essentially a process of qualitative change through the development of the innate capacity of an individual. Attendance at school and the learning-teaching process are means to this end. The desired social and economic changes are the objectives of planned educational system. Thus any socio-economic and cultural changes and progress are the result of the goal-oriented educational planning. While it is agreed upon by the scholars that education is one of the important factors of social change. So, its impact on the development is inevitable. North East India is not exception to this.

Education brings about substantial changes in the socio-economic and cultural life of the people in the State. During the British period there was no developmental infrastructure for North Eastern India. This area was rather allowed to remain isolated from the main stream of Indian life as a matter of policy.

With the emergence of rapid rate of change in the developing and developed countries as a result of new inventions and discoveries in the field of science and technology, the educationists have similarly raised their interest in the study of development. The study of development is at present a common practice among the social scientist like sociologist, anthropologist, economists, educationists, etc. Many a writings can be made available for a detailed discussion on the basic concept of development, but it is beyond the purview of this brief section. Therefore, here an attempt has been made to clarify the operational definition of the concept of development. According to Belshaw, development represents an increase in the capacities of a society to organize for its own objectives, and to carry out its programme more efficiently. He has also examined the impact of education on the society, which to him is both a goal and means. Education in a particular direction may help in the society's estimation of its own performance, and education also creates and channels incentives, personal objectives and occupational skills in the total socio-economic system.

Schumacher has gone a little ahead by saying "Development does not start with goods, it starts with people and their education, organization and discipline". He also said that "Without these three, all resources remain latent, untapped and potential". His views are found more befitting and convincing when we analyses the ultimate outcome of the above three primary factors as emphasized by Schumacher. Every country or society, not matter how devastated, which had a high level of education, organization and discipline brings tremendous development. Education does not jump, it is a gradual process of great subtlety. Organization does not jump; it must circumstance and much the same goes for the discipline, the society like North East cannot be assessed simply through material gains, as material achievement cannot come alone for which definitely people are to become conscious, interested and they are to organize their society and develop suitable educational network in order to establish a permanent set up for the development activities.

Role of Education in Development

The idea that education, at every level, is the key to the abolition of poverty, is described as so revolutionary that if social scientists had more self-confidence they would call it a discovery. The research study concludes that the less developed a society, the smaller the influence of home background on achievement and the greater the effect of school variables. Schooling provides not only basic education, but under the best of circumstances it aids a child to explore the world and to express ideas, ask questions and puzzle out answers. According to the Universal Declaration of Human Rights (Article 26, 1948), schooling is a human right. School education, seeks to prepare the child to live not only in his immediate world but to live in the world beyond his daily experience and thus it provides broader national as well as international view points. This then serve as a mechanism for learning a second culture, or acculturation, which almost invariably means the process of learning a modern culture including science, technology and a world view. On the other hand, there is an internationally held consensus that a common "schooling" experience for a specified period of time is essential for the betterment of mankind individually as well as collectively.

School education develop the basic innate abilities of a person to live a full personal life both as an individual and as a member of a family, and an economically productive life as a worker, and a socially useful life as citizen. The origin of the system of school education which is prevalent today in India can be traced to the beginning of the nineteenth century when the Government of the day had surveys made of the then prevalent systems of the education with a view to reorganizing education to suit the needs of the time. Thus, it reveals that India inherit the British system of school education. The society like North East cannot be developed by adopting the system prevailing in the developed society. In the tribal society the concept of development is inclusive of economic development but differ from it in the sense that it emphasises the development of the totality of the society. On considering the above operational conception of school education, the development of education in North East India has been analysed. For historical reason that region that now constitutes North East India was loosely administered with a little or no accent of educational development. After India's independence the entire area has been brought under the development programmes by the Government.

Education in North-Eastern India Through The Ages

The historical and constitutional documents of North East India reveals that the entire region was with Assam except Manipur and Tripura. There is ample evidence to believe that the region was associated with the country during the Pre-historic period. Thus, looking through the history of the region one can see that the ancient and medieval time the indigenous system of education prevalent in Assam (region) on the one hand and the rest of India on the other hand was similar but not exactly the same. There is no doubt that the pan-Indian system of education in ancient India was mainly Indo-Aryan, sanskrit-oriented. There is no evidence on record whether the non-Aryan indigenous people, who had been living in India prior to the advent of the Aryans, possessed any system of education. Presumedly formal education except the hereditary professional learning, was first introduced by the Aryans who migrated to Pragjyotisha or Kamarupa about the beginning of the Christian era. That any organised indigenous system of education could not be expected in ancient Assam. Historians refer from the Umachal rock inscription of Surendravarman or Mahendravarman that the Indo-Aryans penetrated into North-Eastern India prior to the fifth century A.D. It can be inferred that, the Aryans brought with them the system of education prevalent amongst them. Indo-Aryan learning or more precisely the vedic learning must have been cultivated by a section of Aryanised people of this country even before the fifth century A.D. Nothing is known of the non-Aryan or indigenous system of education if any existed at all. With the advent of the Aryans in Kamarupa, the historians opine that the early rulers of Kamarupa became Aryanised with some high status.

Consequently ancient Assam turned into an indo-Aryan language speaking zone along with their Vedic system of education. Literary sources reveals that the ancient system of education and curriculum as prescribed by the dharma-sutras were also followed in Kamarupa. Instructions were imparted, generally through two fold process. Under the *gurukula* system from the *upanayana* or initiation till the ceremony of *Samavartana* the pupil studied at the house of his teacher and carried on his academic life according to the code of conduct prescribed by the *dharama sutras*. The other agency of transmitting education was the hereditary system where in some used to receive education from their fathers. There was another agency, which has been called *parishad in dharmasastra* continued in western Assam particularly in Kamarupa, till the early decades of 20th century. The duration of study was not less than twelve years to attain mastery. During ancient time holidays were also maintained and the list was prepared in accordance with the auspicious and inauspicious days. There had been no teaching learning on inauspicious days.

The curriculum which was practiced during those days include the Vedas and the ancillary branches, philosophy, etc. as that of the other parts of the country. In addition to that Tantric was practiced in Assam. Kamarupa was recognised as one of the important centres of Tantric learning in Eastern India is adequate proof of the existence of the Tantric education in ancient Assam. But existence of an open system of schooling like other branches of knowledge could not be expected in the case of Tantric system because it was considered as secret affair between the guide and the disciple. Literature (Sanskrit) was popular subject. In addition to that Ayurveda, Jyotisha, Astrology, Art and Craft, Art of dancing both classical and folk, architects, etc. were included in the curriculum. The writing materials in Assam was bark of aguru trees (Acqilaria agolacha) because palm and birch trees were rarely grow in Assam. With the introduction of the script the process of educating pupils became much easier. Bhaskaravarman, the then King of Kamarupa maintain schools or *pathasalas* for spread of education. The Buddhistic education also came down to Assam from Nalanda like that of the emergence of Aryan language script in Assam. The available literature reveals that Buddhistic education which is known as monastic education was in vogue in the North Eastern India. Arunachal Pradesh, particularly Tawang Monastry is the example of the same. In the state of Tripura lot of evidences are available so far Buddhism is concerned, even recent discovery reveals the fact that (in Bengal the bordering area of Eastern India and Assam) the Buddhist monastries are available. So, the existence of monastic education in North Eastern India can not be ruled out.

Formal or institutional education is different branches of learning was generally imparted in *tols*, *catuspathis* and *pathsalas* by gurus or *adhyapakas* in medieval Assam. Education in crafts and arts were either transmitted on hereditary lines or acquired through the medium of professional guilds or Khels, members of which usually settled in the same locality but it had no formal curriculum. The formal education imparted in *tols* and *pathsalas* was not widespread as to cover all section of the population. It was mainly confined to the upper strata of the society. There is no evidence on record that the students belong to other castes were debarred from admission to schools, but their number was extremely limited. Education of women was also there as it is revealed from medieval *carit puthis* or biographical works.

Gurukul system was followed in Assam. No tuition fee was charged. Students used to sit on the ground over which mats of Kusa grass or reeds were usually spread. All the prescriptions of *Dharmasastras* were not followed in toto by pupils of the medieval period. Monitorial system of teaching was in vogue during the period. Such students were called *oja-chatra*. Of course, the people of Assam used to go outside Assam for higher learning. Traditional indigenous knowledge in Art and Craft, Science of medicine, treatment of diseases, architecture were taught and practiced generally on hereditary line. The *satra* institution and its village wing *namghar* served as media of mass education. During late medieval period the *Vaisnavite satras* were patronised by Kings for maintaining schools for teaching boys of the disciples and devotees of the Vaisnavite system. The monastic, semi-monastic, *tols* etc. were maintained.

Sanskrit language, literature, grammar and laxicon, *Smriti, dharamasastra, Vedanta, Mimamsa, Nyaya,* Astrology, Astronomy, Arithmetic, etc. were taught in Assam. Music, dance and musical instruments and various schools of art, architecture designs were learned and practiced by the people. The education was patronised and maintained by the Kings as well as by the voluntary effort of the people. It is reported that some writings were incised in stone slabs and others in copper plates so as to make them permanent. But the usual material on which writing was done was *sachipat*, i.e. bark of agara tree (Aquilaria agallocha). As palm trees do not grow in Assam, palm leaves were not used. Tulapat or country made paper made by pressing cotton pulp was also for writing or coping manuscripts, but such manuscripts are less durable than those written on *sachipat*.[1]

Thus it is evident that the education which was prevailing in Ancient and medieval Assam was indigenous and as well as of the rest of the regions of the country. In the hilly regions of the region of north-east, informal education took place mostly through interaction between children and parents in the family and work place in case of the young. As children grew into adolescence they were attached to local dormitories where they received much of the education and training needed in adult life. These dormitories have been powerful institutions with sanction from the local community and served an important educational function as agencies to impart education for the intellectual and emotional development of youth in the community. They remained active till the advent of the Missionaries into the Region when of beginning was made in the introduction of modern formal system of education in the whole Region (Saika, 1973).

The work of the various Christian Missionaries in the North-Eastern Region is well documented and is known. Among the first Missionary groups to arrive in the region were the American Baptist Mission, the Dutch Baptists, other Presbyterian groups and the Roman Catholics. They came to the interior parts of the region where the people worshipped the forces of nature as Gods and where the hold of superstition was supreme. In many places where the initial groups of Missionaries went they had to face hostility from the local people, and it took them a long time to gain access to the Region and receive acceptability of the people. There followed a period of fruitful interaction between the Missionary groups and the people of the North East Region for the benefit of both. Formal schools were set up in Assam, Meghalaya, Mizoram, Nagaland and in other hilly terrains of the Region. The dialects of the different tribes in the Region were systematically developed into languages like the Khasi, Garo, Bodo, Mizo and the like. The first printing press and the first newspaper in the Region were started by the Missionaries. Alongwith these developments the Christian faith also found its way into the Region. It is the major religion in the Hill States of the Region to-day and is a powerful force of binding people together. Among the non-Christian missionary groups who worked for the educational upliftment of the Region may be made of the Ramakrishna Mission and Vivekananda Society. Both these groups have been actively working among the various tribes of Arunachal Pradesh.

The impact of Missionary efforts on the overall educational development can be seen if one looks at the literacy scene in the different states of the North East Region. Thus the Lushai Hills (the present Mizoram) where the Missionaries started educational work in about 1890 could surpass the All India literacy percentage of about 16 as early as 1931 (Ralte, 1990). The average literacy percentage for the whole of the North East Region minus Arunachal Pradesh was comparable to All India percentage at the time of Independence. The Census figures of 1981 and 1991 indicate that with the exception of Arunachal and Meghalaya all the other states in the North - East Region have continued to maintain the earlier image of advancement in the percentage of literacy as compared to the national average. Mizoram in particular has continued to occupy a place of pride (81.23% of literacy in 1991) next only to Kerala (90.39% in 1991) literacy camp of India (Sachadeva, 1992). The impact of favourable literacy position of the region is not only limited to school education stage alone, but is also visible at the higher stages of education. A recent analysis (Raza and Aggarwal, 1991) of National Sample Survey, reveals that regions with more than 800 persons per one lakh population enrolling are included in all the states in the North East Region with exception of Arunachal Pradesh with the lowest enrolment of 61 persons per one lakh population. In this respect six out of seven states in the region enjoy a status similar to the metropolitan cities of Delhi, Calcutta, Madras and Chandigarh and the West coast region of India.

Primary Education

Universalisation of elementary education, which is a national priority, has three essential ingredients : universal enrolment, minimal drop-outs and enhanced learning achievement not below the Minimum Level of Learning (MLL). In matters of enrolment at primary stage, the states in the region, by and large, are above the national average but in the matter of drop-outs and learning achievement there is a marked disparity between the region and the rest of the country.

The gross-enrolment ratio (GER), as per 6th All India Educational Survey conducted by the NCERT (as on 30th September, 1993) for Class I-V, varies between 92.88 (Assam) to 152.13 (Mizoram) against the national average of 95.32. The GER for class VI-VIII varies between 49.87 (Nagaland) to 76.89 (Manipur) as against the national average of 58.96. The enrolment pattern, though behind the universalization target, is better than the national average in most parts of the region. The situation in respect of drop-outs is however, quite alarming. The following table shows the drop-out rates in 1991-92.

State	*Class I - V*	*I- VIII*	*I - X*
Arunachal Pradesh	59.5	74.9	80.0
Assam	37.8	73.3	78.8
Manipur	67.5	68.5	77.1
Meghalaya	26.7	63.4	85.9
Mizoram	54.8	72.5	70.3
Nagaland	33.2	53.2	70.0
Tripura	62.6	68.7	84.3
India	42.8	57.5	70.3

The drop-out situation in the region is much worse than the rest of the country. Drop-out rates for girls are very high although in terms of average female literacy, the position is better than many other parts of the country.

In matters of learning achievement, the existing situation is a cause for concern. The extremely poor standards for primary education are reflected in secondary and higher education stages as well.

In respect of teachers training, the region is astoundingly deficient. In 1992-93, percentage of untrained teachers varied between 16 (Mizoram) to 67 (Manipur) against the national average of 11 for primary level; 20 (Tripura) to 72 (Assam) middle level; 52 (Mizoram) to 70 (Nagaland) against the national average of 10 for High School level. In terms of numbers, over a lakh teachers in the region are untrained.

The percentage increase in enrolment during 1986-93 as reflected by 6th All India Educational Survey figures in various States in the region is as follows ·

Sl. No.	*State*	*Percentage increase in enrolment in Class*					
		Class I - V		*VI - VIII*		*IX - X*	
		Total	*Girls*	*Total*	*Girls*	*Total*	*Girls*
1.	Arunachal Pradesh	42.52	53.28	85.80	97.23	81.05	123.85
2.	Assam	11.56	16.46	27.14	37.86	38.21	54.40
3.	Manipur	50.40	53.27	53.19	64.57	37.82	51.08
4.	Meghalaya	10.58	10.92	14.14	13.00	00.72	1.95
5.	Mizoram	12.15	11.60	40.81	39.51	36.62	46.32
6.	Nagaland	4.20	5.64	51.48	66.66	53.86	85.42
7.	Tripura	13.96	16.95	11.16	17.90	39.38	44.34
	INDIA	13.08	19.37	24.63	39.19	33.63	53.33

It is apparent that increase in enrolment in percentage term in most of the states in the region is more than the All-India increase. This would require more resources for expansion of the Schools, increase in the number of teachers, more equipments/books/labs/ libraries, etc.

Vocational and technical education could make a viable dent into the problem of educated unemployed in the region but the infrastructural support is grossly inadequate. The institutions for higher education are also inadequate in view of the vast terrain and growing aspirations for higher education although the number of unemployed with higher education is also growing.

For achieving the goal of universalization of elementary education in the North East Region on-going centrally sponsored school improvement related programmes will need special dispensation.

Operation Blackboard

So far, the OB programme has been implemented in 5 out of 7 States. The areas of concern in its effective implementation are:

Under utilisation of funds (e.g. in Meghalaya only 18% of the funds have been spent) substantial number of vacant teachers posts (e.g. in Manipur 278 posts are vacant out of 338 sanctioned) slow pace of construction of school buildings (e.g. 4079 out of 18224 targeted are yet to be constructed in Assam).

Secondary Education

The stage of secondary education and more so of higher secondary education is a terminal stage for some and a transition stage for others. In both the situations this stage turns out to be the most important for the future of an individual. In fact, the grades obtained at this stage more often than not become the crucial deciding factor about whether an individual is going to continue his studies in future or enter the world of work. A detailed description of this stage is therefore warranted from academic, social, and economic considerations. There are about 3607 secondary and 530 Higher Secondary schools in North East.

It is reported in Survey that only 5.87% of the habitations in Arunachal Pradesh, covering 17.38% of the population, were served by secondary sections within eight kilometers. The corresponding percentages according to the survey are 15.72 and 30.61, respectively.

There are only two habitations in the State which are predominantly inhabited by the Scheduled Caste population. While neither has a secondary section within it, both the habitations have the facilities within eight kilometers.

Out of 3,237 habitations in the State, 2,974 (91.88%) are predominantly inhabited by the Scheduled Tribe population. Of these, only 411 (13.82%), covering 23.52% of the population, have access to secondary sections within eight kilometers.

In Assam, the percentage of the habitations served by secondary sections within eight kilometers is 92.83 including 6.11% that have the facilities within the habitations themselves. The corresponding figures in respect of population are 94.88% and 10.67% respectively. It may be mentioned here that these percentages are slightly higher than those in the Fourth Survey.

The State has 1,395 (4.39%) habitations predominantly inhabited by the scheduled caste population. It is observed that slightly more than 90% of them, covering 92.28% of the population, have the facilities for secondary education within eight kilometers.

The State has 6,075 (19.10%) habitations predominantly inhabited by the Scheduled Tribe population. Of these, 4,927 (81.10%) habitations, covering 87.21% of the population, are served by secondary sections within eight kilometers.

It is observed that the percentage of the habitations in Manipur served by secondary sections within eight kilometers is 53.67, which includes 8.19% of the habitations having these facilities within themselves. In terms of population, the corresponding percentages are 73.77 and 20.33, respectively. At the time of the Fourth Survey, the percentage of the habitations served within eight kilometers was 51.13, including 6.87% which had the facilities with themselves. These habitations covered 74.59% and 21.41% of the population, respectively.

There are only 39 (1.49%) habitations predominantly inhabited by the Scheduled Caste population. Of these, 36 (92.31%) habitations covering 95.59% of the population, have the facilities for secondary education within eight kilometers. The percentage of the population, served within the habitations themselves is 31.66.

More than half of the habitations in the State are predominantly inhabited by the Scheduled Tribe population. Of these, 35.17% catering to 45.92% of the population have access to secondary sections within eight kilometers. Further, slightly more than 19% of the population is served within the habitations themselves.

All the 5,337 habitations in the State of Meghalaya are predominantly inhabited by the Scheduled Tribe population. A significant increase in the facilities for schooling at the secondary stage has been noticed in the period between the Fourth and the Fifth Survey. According to the Fifth survey, 54.79% of the habitations, covering 61.31% of the population, have the facilities for secondary educations within eight kilometers. The corresponding figures at the time of the Fourth Survey were 43.66% and 51.94% respectively. Further, the percentage of the population served within the habitations now is 11.08 as against 5.92 in 1978.

There are 616 habitations with a population of 4,29,372 in Mizoram. All of them are predominantly inhabited by the Scheduled Tribe population. The percentage of the population served by secondary sections within eight kilometers is 67.76 as against 63.32 at the time of the Fourth Survey. It is interesting to note that 58.12% of the total population in rural areas has these facilities within the habitations themselves.

In Nagaland all the 997 habitations are predominantly inhabited by the Scheduled Tribe population. Of these, 27.58% covering 43.09% of the rural population have access to secondary sections within eight kilometers. The corresponding percentages at the time of the Fourth Survey were 31.24 and 44.39, respectively. Further, 14.31% of the rural population is served by secondary sections within the habitations themselves.

At the time of the Fourth Survey, 58.37% of the habitations in Tripura, covering 75.44% of the population, had the facilities for secondary education within eight kilometers. These percentages have considerably increased during the period 1978 - 86. According to the Fifth Survey figures, the percentage of the habitations served within eight kilometers is 83.37 and their population is 93.62% of the total population in rural areas in the State.

There are 779 (12.37%) habitations predominantly inhabited by the Scheduled Caste population. Almost all (97.56%) of them are served by secondary sections within a distance of eight kilometers.

A majority (62.95%) of the total number of habitation in the State are predominantly inhabited by the Scheduled Tribe population. Nearly three-fourths of them, covering 82.99% of the population, have the facilities for secondary education within eight kilometers.

Non Formal Education (NFE)

The Non-Formal Education (NFE) programme is being implemented by only 3 states in the region viz., Assam, Manipur and Mizoram. There are only 12 voluntary agencies in Assam, 2 in Manipur and nine in Mizoram. In Assam, very old NFE material is being used which need thorough revision. The NFE primers in Manipur are not based on minimum levels of learning (MLLs). There is no NFE teaching-learning material in Mizoram. The NFE feedback reporting from the states is also inadequate.

The focus of the centrally sponsored NFE scheme is on the ten educationally backward states. However, it has been extended to cover urban slums, hilly tribal and desert areas and areas with concentration of working children. Although Arunachal Pradesh is an educationally backward state, yet it has not opted to avail the central assistance under NFE.

The NFE methodology has potential to play a crucial role in achieving the goal of UEE. The North East states may consider this system as a suitable educational intervention for those children in the age group 6-14 who are unable to participate in the Formal Education system due to certain constraints. The NCERT has provided resource support for development of curricula and instructional material and training of personnel.

Extension of District Primary Education Programme (DPEP) in all the North East states, is focussed on District Planning and location specific interventions for Primary education development. The criteria for selection of the Districts under DPEP are :

- Educationally backward Districts with a female literacy rate below the national average (39.2% as per 1991 Census)

- Districts where Total Literacy Campaigns (TLCs) have been successful leading to enhanced demand for Elementary education.

District-wise position based on the above criteria for the North East states is as follows.

Sl. No.	*Name of the State*	*Total No. of Districts*	*Districts with female literacy rate below the national average*
1.	Arunachal Pradesh	11	11
2.	Assam	20	4
3.	Manipur	8	3
4.	Meghalaya	5	2
5.	Mizoram	3	1
6.	Nagaland	7	1
7.	Tripura	3	1

Although in terms of average female literacy the position is better in the North East states than many other parts of the country but drop-out rates for girls at primary stage of schooling are very high and need to be addressed.

At present only 8 districts of Assam are covered under the DPEP in the North East region. The DPEP may be extended to other seven states of the region through domestic resources.

Vocational Education

The scheme of Vocational Education has not been effectively utilised by the States in the North East and in some States it is yet to take off. Out of the sanctioned vocational sections only Assam, Manipur and Mizoram have operationalised the scheme. The other States are yet to operationalise the scheme. Management structures at State, SCERT and district levels have been created only in the

States of Assam and Manipur. However, a very few posts are filled. At school level also some posts of part-time and full-time teachers are filled in Assam, Manipur and Mizoram. District surveys have partly been conducted in Assam and Mizoram only.

The North East States have recommended that :

- Establishment of a Regional vocational Training Centre to coordinate the research and training component of vocationalisation of education be centrally-funded. The Training Centre may be established as an integral part of NERIST at Itanagar.

- Suitable measures be taken to facilitate ultimate self-employment of vocational education passed-outs by establishing necessary linkages with financial institutions and imparting vocational education in limited location and area-specific streams.

Steps for Development of Vocational Education

The North Eastern Council has observed that a common institution like the North-Eastern Regional Institute of Vocational Education (NERIVE) can be set up in a phased manner by active involvement of all the States in region provided following could be ensured:

- Adequate number of teachers in vocational education at plus-two stage are available for training by the Institute.

- Whether these trained teachers would get adequate facility for development of vocational education after joining their parent departments. Whether the State will be able to bear the recurring expenditure in connection with running of the institute.

The NCERT has planned to operationalize its Regional Institute of Education for the North-East in 1995. One of the Division of the Institute will be Vocational Education. The main function of this Division will be identification survey of need-based vocational programmes, development of course curriculum including textual material and teacher training. It will assist the State in the region in starting vocational streams in senior secondary schools and with the vocationalisation of the secondary education.

Based on the experiences gained in the implementation of Vocational Education Programme and as several States/UTs are not able to meet their liabilities, particularly on salary, Govt. of India has decided to provide 100% funds for created posts (about 50%) at different levels. This should enable the State Govts. in the region to create management structure at all level and also make available other infrastructural and academic facilities for smooth implementation of the programme.

Adult Education

Literacy figures for the states in the region and for the country as a whole in 1991 are as follows :

State	% of literacy
Arunachal Pradesh	41.59
Assam	52.89
Manipur	59.89
Meghalaya	49.10
Mizoram	82.27
Nagaland	61.65
Tripura	60.44
India	52.21

Although many states may have higher literacy percentage than the national average the need for strengthening adult education efforts is obvious. TLC campaigns have been sanctioned in seven districts of Assam and in all the three districts of Tripura. These need to be taken up in all other states as well. Since it is difficult to launch TLC in the rural areas as the colleges are located in limited urban centres, the centre based approach for AE should be allowed to continue in the region.

Promotion of Hindi

A working group on the North East had recommended that :

"The group unanimously felt that in order to accelerate the process of national integration and to promote gradual voluntary acceptance of the official language of the Union, large allocation should be made for the schemes relating to appointment of Hindi teachers and promotion of Hindi".

The Department of Education has the following two schemes for the development of Hindi :

1. Appointment and training of Hindi teachers in non-Hindi speaking states/UTs.

2. Scheme of financial assistance to voluntary organizations for promotion of Hindi.

Under the scheme (1) above, 100% financial assistance is provided for salary of Hindi teachers appointed with the prior approval of the Government of India for one plan only and for strengthening / establishment of Hindi Teachers Training Colleges. Although 140 Hindi teachers have been promoted during VIIIth Plan, the demand for appointment of more Hindi teachers are not being made due to inadequate Budget allocation.

Under scheme (2) above, 37 agencies were funded with an amount of 90.46 lakhs during 1994-95.

The inadequacy of funds should not be allowed to come in the way of development of Hindi in the region.

Higher Education

All the seven States of North-East, except Mizoram have either State or Central Universities. There is one Central University in the region namely North-Eastern Hill University at Shillong. During 1994 three Central Universities namely Assam, Tezpur and Nagaland were notified. The Acts of parliament setting up the Assam and Nagaland Universities, which had been lying unimplemented since 1989, have been finally given effect in 1994. The total number of colleges imparting higher education in this region are 327 out of which 191 colleges are recognized by UGC under Section 2(f) of UGC Act to receive grant from the Commission. The applications of only 3 more colleges for seeking recognition under Section 2(f) of UGC Act are currently pending with the Commission, whereas, 133 colleges have not yet applied for recognition. Indira Gandhi National Open University (IGNOU) also has one of its Regional

Centres at Shillong to cater to the need of this region in respect of Distance Education. IGNOU is offering its programmes in the region since 1988 and is able to attract approximately 3000 students in a year.

Surveys on enrolment pattern at the tertiary level shows that majority of the students enrolled into undergraduate and post-graduate courses in the North Eastern region are in Arts stream. The dependence on Arts education at the tertiary level has created both shortages and surplus of different categories of manpower. Therefore, there is a need to develop science and professional courses in the universities.

Recommendations

The North East States have Recommended that:

1. Need-based centrally funded programme to enable expansion of existing colleges.

2. More UGC funded colleges under relaxed norms to enable students to secure higher education outside urban centres.

3. Establishing UGC facilities in the North East Region for enabling college teachers to undergo prescribed professional advancement programmes.

4. Setting up of the North Eastern Region Centre of the UGC on priority to enable UGC to concentrate attention on the educational inadequacies of the region. The UGC Regional Centre has virtually established in Guwahati.

Steps Taken

Following steps have been taken by the Government for the promotion of higher education in this region:

1. Government has conveyed approval, in principle, for establishment of a Post-Graduate Centre of the North Eastern Hill University at Tura. To begin with, it has been decided to introduce PG Course in Economics and Mathematics in that Centre. The Centre would be further developed during the 9th plan.

2. The question of establishment of a Central University in Mizoram is under consideration. The tentative view of the Government is, subject to the approval of the Planning Commission, that earmarked outlays in the State Plan may be provided for establishment of a State University in Mizoram.

3. The University Grants Commission's branch office for the North Eastern Region at Guwahati is likely to become functional soon.

4. Pending application of 3 Colleges seeking recognition under Section 2(f) of UGC Act will be decided on merits by July 31, 1995. Special Arrangements will also be made for UGHC nominees to visit the 133 colleges of North-East region who have not applied for recognition under Section 2(f), with a view to getting their application filled up and submitted to the UGC for a decision by the Commission of merits and this task shall be completed in a time-bound manner. Efforts will be made to complete the entire process by December 31, 1995.

Technical Education

To cater for technical manpower requirements of the North Eastern States under the Joint Venture of Centre and States, Regional Engineering College (REC) at Silchar in Assam was established more than a decade ago. At Silchar, students of the seven sister states are admitted on the Centralised Entrance Examination conducted by the Directorate of Technical Education, Government of Assam. Seats in other 16 RECs are also provided to the students who qualify from North East States, based upon the population.

North Eastern Regional Institute of Science and Technology (NERIST), Nirjul, Itanagar, Arunachal Pradesh is currently conducting 19 courses at different levels namely 6 at certificates, 6 at diploma and 7 at degree levels with intake of 30 students of each level. According to the admission policy of the institute, 90% of the seats are meant for students residing in the North-East Region. Each State is represented on the Board of Management of this institute.

Government of India has established an IIT at Guwahati in Assam in 1994. The admission process for the IIT has started through the JEE 1995-96 session. Besides (these technical education institutions), there are three other Engineering Colleges and twenty five diploma level institutions in the North Eastern States. There are 16 Community Polytechnics in North East Region for the states : Assam (8), Manipur (2), Meghalaya (1), Mizoram (1), Nagaland (1), Tripura (1). There is no Polytechnic in Arunachal Pradesh. During the years 1993-94 to 1994-95, 3 Polytechnics in the North Eastern Region including Sikkim have been covered under the scheme of Community Polytechnics. AICTE has approved the establishment of community Polytechnic in Imphal during 1995-96.

Assam State has been covered under the World Bank Scheme of Technician Education in its second phase i.e. during January 1992. An allocation of Rs. 300 million has been made for this State under the scheme.

Besides the seats allocated in RECs and reservation in NERIST students of North East Region states seats in Engineering and Diploma level courses are also allocated by Government of India. The Government of India allocates seats from one State/UT to the other State/UT in the field of Engineering/Technology in areas of which are either not available or State/UT is lacking in facilities in these areas. Under this scheme special consideration is given to the North Eastern States. Nearly 50% seats of the total available are allocated to these States.

The total number of seats in RECs including REC Silchar for students from the North-East States is 151

Recommendations

The North East States have Recommended that:

1. One more Regional Engineering College be established in the North East Region to cater for the technical manpower requirements of the North East States whose development is handicapped for want of technical personnel,

2. To bridge the gap, till such time as the additional Regional Engineering College is established, the quota of engineering seats allotted to hilly States of the North East Region be adequately increased.

Teacher Education

In respect of teachers education, the region is astounding deficient. In 1992-93, percentage of untrained teachers varied between 16 (Mizoram) to 67 (Tripura) against the national average of 11 for primary level ; 20 (Tripura) to 72 (Assam) middle level; 52 (Mizoram) to 70 (Nagaland) against the national average of 10 for High School level. In terms of numbers, over a lakh teachers in the region are untrained.

The percentage of trained primary teachers in the North East region varies from 34 (Tripura) to 67 (Assam). In the case of upper primary teachers, it ranges from 26 (Nagaland) to 75 (Mizoram).

The North East region has over 90000 untrained teachers. However, the region has only 22 elementary training institutes for conducting preservice training programmes. 38 out of 61 districts in region have been sanctioned the District Institutes of Education and Training (DIETS). While DIETs have been sanctioned in all the districts of Assam and Meghalaya, only 1 out of 11 districts in Arunachal Pradesh have been sanctioned DIETs. Only one fifth of the total posts in DIETs (170 out of 881 sanctioned) have been filled up. Given the criticality of providing a sound institutional base for sustained teachers training, both preservice and in-service, speedy operationalisation of sanctioned institutions may be done.

No much emphasis has been given for the growth of secondary education before independence in North Eastern region. It was only after 1826 the modern system of Teacher Education started in North East For teachers of secondary schools, St.Edmund's and St. Mary's Colleges at Shillong were providing training (B.T. course). These institutions continued to run on aided basis. The course in teaching organised by St.Edmund's was discontinued when the department of teacher's training (B.T) was started in 1949 by the University of Guwahati. St. Mary's College at Shillong used to admit lady teachers joining the college on their own. Rapid growth of secondary teacher education in North Eastern Region has been observed during the last decade. Now there are 63 colleges for secondary teacher education in the North Eastern Region.

The growth of secondary teacher education in pre-independence period was very limited. In the post-independence period the growth has been noticed satisfactorily. The State Governments followed a progressive policy for the development of education always shifting emphasis from quantitative to qualitative improvement. The implementation of different schemes under the five year plans contributed greatly to the promotion and development of education at various stages in the North East. In the recent past there has been a rapid increase in number of training institutions. But the inadequate and ineffective supply of trained teachers is still a problem engaging the attention of the academicians and of the authorities of the states.

A qualitative teaching-learning situation is expected to promote the societal environment as well as to meet the national goal. The effective and qualitative aspect of teaching-learning depends upon the competent teachers. In this connection, the role of secondary teacher education colleges are distinguished.

SCERTs

So far only Mizoram has been granted central assistance for strengthening of SCERT. Financial assistance for upgradation of SCERTs was provided during 1995-96 to Assam and Nagaland.

Regional Institute of Education (RIE)

The NCERT had set up a Regional Institute of Education (RIE) to provide academic and technical resource support to state and district level institutions in the North East region to tackle specific educational needs of the states in the region.

Institute of Advanced Study in Education (IASE)

For further augmentation of the resource base for the North East region in the field of School Education including elementary and secondary stages, it established an Institute of Advanced

Studies in Education (IASE) at the North - East Hill University. This institution in coordination with RIE (NCERT), IGNOU and CIIL Regional office take up pre-service post-graduate level teacher education programmes.

The North Eastern Region has made great stride with regard to quantitative expansion of education at all stages. While the trend in this direction should continue, efforts are also be made to imporove the quality of education. And to develop education on the lines which take note of its present deficiencies and also take care to the emerging needs of the region.

The political division of the parent State of Assam into several states has given the Regional Units an opportunity to develop on lines best suited to their geniuses and needs. This is a step towards democratic decentralization giving real power to the people to shape their own destinies within a Federal setup.

The parent State of Assam received special attention during the various plan periods to set up facilities for professional studies within its territory, since these were common facilities, the State of Assam has been accommodating students from the various North Eastern States into its instututions. Efforts have also been made to reserve some seats for students from the Hill States in various professional courses located in different parts of the country.

These are at best temporary measures and can not meet the ever increasing demand for professional studies of students from the Region. One of the urgent needs of the Region is to increase the need to identify newer areas of study and research for which facilities will have to be developed in the Region itself. These are challenges for the planners and adminstrators of the Region and they need to be taken seriously if the Region has to develop in an all-round manner.

REFERENCES

Bhattacharjee, J.B. Sequence of Development in North-East-India, Anomol publisher, New Delhi, 1989.

Biswas, N.B., Education in Arunachal Pradesh; A Historical Profile, Arunachal Review, Vol - IV, No. 7, 1992.

Basic Statistics of North Eastern Region, 1995, North Eastern Council, Shillong.

Census Reports, 1931 to 1991, Govt. of India.

Elwin Verrier, Philosophy for NEFA, Shillong 1951

Ering, D. North-East Frontier Agency, in the Tribal Situation in India, Ed. by K.Suresh Singh, Motilal Banarsidass, Delhi, 1972.

Gokulanathan, P.P., Education in North-East India Through the years, Journal on NEIES, Vol- I, Shillong, 1992.

Godfrey, H., Quoted on "Education as Key to Abolition of Poverty" from Gunnar Myrdal, Asian Drama, New Delhi, Kalyani Publisher, 1982.

Raza, M. (Ed), Higher Education in India : Retrospect and Prospect, AIU, New Delhi, 1991.

Saikia, S., History of Education in India, Mani Manik Prakash, Guwahati, 1973.

Sarma, S.N., Education, in the Comprehensive History of Assam, (Ed) Vol-I, H.K. Barpujari, Publication Board, Guwahati, 1994.

Sarma, S.N., Language, Literature and Education in the Comprehesive History of Assam, Vol-III, (Ed). H.K. Barpujari, Publication Board Assam, Guwahati, 1994.

Sachdeva, J.L., Working Paper Presented at North East Zone, the Conference on Adult Education at Shillong, 1992.

Schumacher, E.F., Small is Beautiful, Radhakrishna, New Delhi, 1972.

Sixth All India Educational Survey Report, NCERT, New Delhi, 1995.

Yonuo, A., The Rising Naga - A Historical and Political Study, Vivek Publishing House, Delhi, 1974.

II

EDUCATION IN ARUNACHAL PRADESH

A Historical Perspective

Arunachal - the abode of Sun's rays. This is the enchanting land with sprawling mountains, turbulent rivers. evergreen forests, deep valleys, beautiful plateaus. Arunachal Pradesh, situated on the extreme north-east of India is 83,743 sq km in area and has a long international border with Bhutan to the west (160 km), China to the north and north-east (1030 km) and Burma to the east, (440). It stretches from snow-caped mountains in the north to the plains of Brahmaputra valley in the south. Arunachal is an ancient land and references of the land occur in the literature of the *Kalika Purana, The Mahabharata, The Ramayana, Sankhyayana Grihya Sanghrah,* etc. This land is a myriad of very simple, hardy and hospitable tribes. There are 110 tribes and sub-tribes. speaking some fifty to sixty different dialects - belonging to Tibeto-Burman and Tai group of languages. Arunachal is acknowledged to be one of the most splendid and multilingual tribal area of the world

For many decades, Arunachal Pradesh remained inaccessible and hidden, remote and unknown to other parts of the country. The history of the administration of present Arunachal Pradesh may be traced back to the Government of India's Notification of 1914 when some tribal areas of Assam's Darrang and Lakhimpur districts were united to form the North-East Frontier Tract (NEFT). The NEFT was further sub-divided into the Balipara Frontier Tract, Lakhimpur Frontier Tract, Sadiya Frontier Tract and the Tirap Frontier Tract during various stages of evolution between 1914 and 1946. These Frontier Tracts, together with the Naga Tribal area, were collectively renamed the North-East Frontier Agency (NEFA) in 1951.

Again in 1954, the NEFA was reconstituted into the Kameng, Subansiri, Tirap, Siang, Lohit and Tuensang Frontier Divisions. However, in 1957, the Tuensang Frontier Division was separated from the then NEFA and merged with the newly constituted Naga Hills Tuensang Area (present Nagaland), the other five divisions in due course became the original districts. These districts have been further sub-divided with the passage of time, and the state presently has twelve districts.

Arunachal Pradesh acquired an independent political status only in 1972 when it was upgraded as a Union Territory. The territory ceased to be a tribal area within the state of Assam. In 1986, the Government of India conferred statehood on this Union Territory. Thus, the endeavor which began hesitatingly in the early part of this century has ripened into maturity in the fullness of time.

Development in Education: An Interaction

Traditional societies which desire to modernize themselves have to transfer their educational system before trying to expand it, because the greater the expansion of the traditional system of education, the more difficult and costly it becomes to change its character. This truth has been lost sight of and, during recent years, we have greatly expanded a system which continues to have essentially the same features it had at its creation about a century ago[1]. Arunachal Pradesh particularly during NEFA did not inherit any system of education of its own. Rather the system of education which was in vogue in the other part of the country was transplanted in the then NEFA. India spread the British traditional bequeathal education throughout the country and Arunachal is not an exception to it. Education is an integrated growth. It is life, and life is a chain of continuous growth. This growth of education is the outcome of the interplay and intertwining of various forces such as socio-economic and political. There is no single factor which could be isolated and specifically mentioned as being responsible for the growth of education at a particular place and a particular given period. The history of the development of education in Arunachal Pradesh is of great significance from the standpoint of the study of the change and movement of the society. It is perhaps the only territory where neither the British took any step to introduce education nor the people. This is the land where India could have started its experiment for evolving the original system of education for the country. Because the land was a hidden one, neither ancient nor medieval or beginning of the modern system of education had marked any influence there prior to Indian independence. So, the basic questions like what would have been the education in India if the Britishers did not come to India ? Or whether India has evolved its own system of education after independence or it has inherited the British system of traditional education are not pertinent in Arunachal Pradesh. Although we often speak of a special education for Arunachal, there has in fact been little to distinguish its schools from the conventional schools of the plains.

The present researcher is of firm conviction that the development of education during the period under study (1918-1991) were directly or indirectly the outcome of the interaction of socio-economic and political factors. This would be amply shown in the subsequent sections.

The political development in the State has had its inevitable reaction on its educational system. Arunachal Pradesh, until 1972 known as North East Frontier Agency, often abbreviated NEFA since 1954, remained inaccessible and hidden. Nothing is known definitely about the conditions prevailing in the area till the 18th century. NEFA started administrative functioning as early as in 1882. So the information may be available from that period onwards. So many administrative changes were made in the territory since 1882 to 1954 and also upto 1972. It used to be administered by the Governor of Assam as agent to the President of India till 1972. In 1972 it got the status of Union Territory by the name Arunachal

Pradesh and then in 1987 it has achieved its statehood. Thus the growth and development of education must be studied as per the requirements of the then administration as well as the interplay of the people. Though it is difficult to isolate any of the factors, like social, economic and political from education, it is possible to see the inter-relationship between one of these and of education. The growth of education is to be interpreted against the background of the policies evolved. "Education does not proceed in a vacuum, its character is determined by the group culture and schools, institutions created by society to attain certain specific ends"[2]. Thus it is easy to point out that since education is something that takes place in the society, for the society and by the society, this changing nature of cultural aspect is vital. If education is a creative force it must make some initiative and responsibility for social progress. If the education is to be dynamic, it must reflect the social growth. Social movements make changes in educational provision, methods, administration and curricula imperative. Thus, one can see that education and society are inter-linked. While education maintains the continuity of the physical and the social life it conserves social heritage and culture and also recognizes, reconstructs and improve human society. Society also plays a vital role in the development of education. Rather it is the product of variety of factors that characterize the life of people. Some of the factors like racial, religious, cultural and economic and political have been responsible for shaping the educational pattern. "In view of this situation, it is probably not extravagant to claim that education is primarily a social process which constitutes one of the main dimensions of any philosophy of education"[3]. The economic factors are also at the root of the growth of education. The economic standard of living and the general poverty or richness of a society affects education. Education can modify the economic system. Thus education and economic development are inter-related. Thus, the growth of education cannot be understood unless economic factors are taken cognizance of. The present study has been conducted on considering the above factors. Of course detailed analyses were not presented because it will increase the volume of the book and size of the chapter. However, the author has presented the relationship of education and development in the first section of the chapter which is followed by the section-role of school education in development process and with the development of school education in Arunachal Pradesh - a trend analysis and critical review of the same.

A Historical Profile

The area known as Arunachal Pradesh is a highly green land of simple people belonging to 110 tribes and sub-tribes. We have practically no material written or unwritten, relating to the history as well as education of this area other than some oral literature. Many writers from outside and within, have written books, pamphlets and articles on Arunachal Culture and writings have been printed and published by Government of Arunachal Pradesh from time to time. But it is a matter of regret that none of the publications highlights any stage of education in Arunachal Pradesh such as what it was and how the present formal system of education came up. In order to make the beginning in this process the present investigation has been conducted. The information was collected from primary as well as from the secondary sources. Since the territory was hidden to the people of India during the ancient and medieval period, the people of the area might have been leading the primitive life. Education might be absent till the time of the unvailed of the land.

The system of formal education in particular had been conspicuously absent in the past in Arunachal Pradesh. Except the Buddhists, the system of even informal education had been non-existent. It is traced that among the Monpas who were highly concentrated to the North-West portion of the Kameng district, the mythological education used to be imparted through Monastery. The people of this area is known as Monpa. Monpas are Buddhists and had trade relations with Tibet, Assam and Bhutan. The Buddhist monastery at Tawang is possibly one of the largest in India. Except the Khamtis in Lohit District the Monpas are the only people who can claim to have a script of their dialect, Monpa. The Library in the Tawang monastery can boast of a large number of books almost all of which are in manuscript. The rest of the non-Buddhist tribes in Arunachal Pradesh do not have their own script. Thus it can be assumed that while the people had their relation with Tibet and Bhutan and are Buddhists in religion naturally the impact of Monastic education might have been there, thus the system of education was practically that of the Buddhist order or Samgha.

Monastic Education

Tawang monastery is the oldest and biggest of the kind in India. This monastery is the centre of wisdom of the spiritual life of the Monpas, the followers of Buddhism in Tawang. It is situated on a hillock about 2 kms west of Tawang township, overlooking the Tawang valley, rivers and mountains surrounding it. Tawang monastery could be seen from a long distance, standing like a white fort, guarding its inmates from external hostilities. The founder of this famous monastery was Ladore Gyatso, popularly known as Mera Lama, who was born in pondung household in Kitpi village of Tawang district. He received his education in the monasteries of Tashilhunpo, Sera and Gyume (Lhasa, Tibet). The monastery, its full name Tawang Galdan Namgyelhatse was instituted. The exact date and year of its construction is not known precisely, even then, it is said to be built around 1643 to 1647, i.e. more than 350 years ago. The monastery has a capacity of accommodating about five hundred monks.

Mode of Admission to the Monastery

The admission to the monastery is generally sought from the families who are having more than three sons, it is usually the second or middle son of the family, but if they want it, they can admit the third son to the monastery. The system of education in the monastery is somewhat, resembles to that of a Gurukul system of education. There is no formal system of classes for the pupils like the modern education. Rather they receive the education under the guidance of their respective monks or tutor in their own dormitory or residence.

While admitting, the parents engage one of the senior monks of the monastery as their tutor for their sons. If they are having any relative among the resident monks then the parents can put their son under his guidance as a novice. Thus, the parents get the boy's head shaved, put on monks attire and then take him to the guru.

The guru takes the boy on the following day to the assembly hall (*dukhang*) and conveys the desire of the boy and his parents for ordination to the monastic order. The guru then offers a ceremonial scarf to the abbot (head lama) and seek his approval for the boy's admission and ordination to the order. The abbot performs ordination ceremony according to the prescribed text and bestows on the boy a religious name and thus from now onward, he will be known by that name. The changing of the boy's name signifies the detachment from the family life and worldly pleasures. Now the boy becomes a fully ordained novice, a member of religious community and his life belongs to the monastery. He lives in the residence of his guru and there he receives his education. The guru teaches the novice (*genin*) in his dormitory. First, he is familiarised with the basic letters of the alphabets, the script used is that of Tibetan script. He is also taught the elementary of the religious text, etc.

Promotion to Higher Grades

When several pupils complete the basic knowledge, they are promoted to higher grade called *getsul*. It is usually done on an auspicious day. The candidates are presented to the abbot; the abbot will read out from the religious text called *getsul* while performing the rites or ceremony. After that, the pupil becomes *getsul*. He now studies the sacred text in the method of various rituals and religious ceremonies etc. When the *getsul* attains the age of 21 years or so, he is accorded a higher grade once more i.e. *gelong* by the abbot. Here also the abbot (head lama) will perform the prescribed rituals and ceremonies. Thus, the monastic order includes all these three grades, *genin* (pupil), *getsul* and *gelong*, and the member of the order is known as *dapa* i.e., fully ordained monk.

The monk or gelong who wishes for the advanced studies may go to the famous monasteries of Drepong, Sera and Gyudmed monasteries in Tibet during those days. Some of the brigl ter monks are deputed to look after the *gompa* (temple) in villages which are under the jurisdiction of Tawang Monastery. They are thus attached to those *gompas* for a period of nine years consecutively in three gompas, i.e., three years in each *gompa*. The monk will be caretaker of that *gompa* and performs connected religious functions and rituals ceremonies.

Review of Monastic Education

Monastic system of education did not offer any educational opportunities independently of its monasteries. All education, sacred as well as secular, was in the hands of the monks. Education was mostly confined to those who used to dedicate their life to serve the society through Monastery. It is necessary to make it clear that the Buddhist of Arunachal have their scripts with the prime purpose of reading religious scriptures. The application of scripts for other than religious purpose was almost absent. The documentation-practice remained totally absent in the territory in the past. The whole tribal society in Arunachal Pradesh remained verbal in the past.

Emergence of Formal Education

The real beginning of formal education was made during 1947 when two lower primary schools were started with 100 enrolment comprising both boys and girls. Since then there has been rapid development in the field of education except the years 1957-58. A sharp fall in the number of school took place during the above years due to consolidation and conversion of the primary schools into inter-village schools. The transfer of the erstwhile Frontier Division of Twensang to Naga Hills now known as Nagaland also contributed in this regard. However, the opening of schools in the territory continued to make steady progress year after year subsequently.

Languages

Nature has itself played a significant role in the evolution of tribal languages in the hills of Arunachal as else where. There are about sixty speech communities which can be broadly grouped into twenty four major language groups. Linguistically, the Adis inhabiting the Siang Districts and the Tagins, Nishis, Hill Miris, Apatanis inhabiting the Subansiri Districts may be classified under one group.

According to the linguistic survey of India, they are classified under the North Assam group of the Tibeto-Burman family. In some language areas, again there are some linguistic islands, such as Soha in the Namsang-Nocte area of Tirap District and Lish in the Central Monpa area of Kameng District. The efforts are being made to develop a common script for the people of the state.

A Spirit of Indianization of Education

One of the main objectives of education is to preserve and transmit the heredity and culture to the next generation subject to modification. The spirit of Indianization sprang in the minds of Indians and it was free in the case of the people of the hilly areas like Arunachal Pradesh for all-round development identity.

There are different views of the different schools of thought as regards to the Indianization of education. But most of them agree to one major point that the replacement of Indian approach in India, instead of British grafting is indeed the best system of education for the Indians. But recently after the report of Indian Education Commission or Kothari Commission report of 1964-66, the people changed their mind to English Education—systematically the style and approach to the extent is said to be English.

This approach and methods were accepted particularly in the hill areas and Arunachal Pradesh is not exceptional to this. Under this circumstance of the changing spirit and environment, the Arunachal Pradesh people also preferred to English style of education in its approach, method, curriculum, text book, etc. like other hill states.

English teaching from Kindergarten to College lėvel is a must in Arunachal and the Hindi language is regarded as the second language. However, the government is lacking much more care for the development of education right from the pre-primary onwards.

The Indianization of Education has the following objectives:

(a) Child is the centre of teaching;

(b) Education should be activity and craft centred;

(c) Productive approach;

(d) Sense of dignity of manual labour;

(e) Medium of instruction being mother tongue;

(f) Co-relation of subject and work;

(g) Idea of truth and non-violence; and

(h) Last but not the least the work for social upliftment in collective effort.

The psychological aspect of learning by doing channelizing the surplus energy and the very important point to keep in mind is "a learner learns what he learns and what he does".

The learning is not attractive and not motivating for the pupils. Today, education is with less impression of the teaching and other economic, social reasons at the root of pushing them to stagnation and wastage and least percentage of literacy.

The spirit of Indianization gets no recommendation in the state of Arunachal Pradesh due to obvious reasons remained untouched even in the present environment.

The recommendation of the different committees in respect to educational development and rational in balance is self explanatory in its objectives and achievement.

Indigenous System of Education

Arunachal Pradesh was a "state of darkness" till 1947, till attainment of independence. Almost the entire population was illiterate and there was not a single educational institution in the state. Though it was an arduous task to penetrate the area with the light of education, yet no attempt was made by the British rulers.

Arunachal Pradesh had no vernacular language during the pre-British period. No doubt, that the Mompas and khamtis had script of their own but were restricted to their own geographical areas only. The Adis say that the ancestors of the Mompas, Khambas and the Tamis was the brothers. The wiseman once gave them (Mompas, Khambas and Tamis) scripts inscribing the history, culture, and civilization of the human race. While the scripts of Mompas and Khambas were written in stone slates, the script of Tanis were written on animal skin. One day when the Tani felt hungry he burnt it and ate it. So the Adis say that Tanis have no script but they have a very sharp memory till today.

During the pre-British period the system of education was mostly oral. The fathers, who had frequent movement to the border areas of Assam markets, imparted education to sons through mouths. The history, culture and civilization of the people was thus transformed from one generation to another through mouth alone.

Missionary Efforts in Education in NEFA till 1947

Arunachal Pradesh (erstwhile NEFA) is the only area where the Missionaries could not penetrate directly even in the British regime. But the activities of the Missionaries was in full swing from the base organization which are in the Arunachal-Assam borders. In 1946, Rev. and Mrs. K.W. Hang Strom set up a Mission School near North Lakhimpur town of Assam in which few Nishi children were enrolled. The British government was satisfied by opening only four Primary schools in the foot hill areas of NEFA (erstwhile Balipara Frontier Tract).

There are cases when boys of Arunachal went to Nagaland, Assam and Meghalaya for study in school and colleges. Of course, the Missionaries could not start any Missionary school in Arunachal Pradesh, perhaps due to imposition of Innerline Act.

Education in Post-Independent Arunachal (1947-72)

The question of education is vital to any comprehensive scheme of development, it was much so in NEFA when the tribes except the Khamtis lacked a script. In the case of Khamtis who migrated from the direction of Burma have their own script which derived from the Tai language. A few literate Mompas of the Kameng district could, of course, read the Tibetan scripts, but such literacy was confined to a few Lamas of the Tawang Lamasery. It is not difficult to see, therefore, that the NEFA Administration had a tremendous task in building up from the scratch so far as education was concerned. It is practically the only area in north-east India where the Missionaries had not been around, and the British Government had not content with starting only four lower primary schools prior to 1947 and were located in the foot hills (erstwhile Balipara Frontier Tract). In the nature of things, therefore, education proved to be the corner stone around which to build the edifice of a prosperous life for the tribal population and at the same time secure their participation in the progress of the land.

When India became free in 1947, Arunachal Pradesh (erstwhile North East Frontier Tract) was made the part of Assam. But the Assam Government also neglected education in Arunachal Pradesh. Arunachal Pradesh made a humble beginning in the field of educational growth only when North-East Frontier Agency, popularly known as NEFA was carved out of Assam with its Headquarters at Shillong amidst wide criticisms in Assam. The real development in education was accelerated in Arunachal Pradesh when she was made a Uninon Territory in 1972. In the same year the medium of education in Arunachal Pradesh became English in place of Assamese.

Though the achievement in the field of education was no small yet the NEFA administration had to face severe criticism from time to time from different quarters on account of its vacillation and indecision. It was also accused from time to time of politicking, particularly on the question of medium of instruction, depending on the particular time was in the helm of affairs in the department of education. One Director of Education was manhandled at least on two occasions on the sensitive question of medium of instruction.

In the month of September 1947, the Department of Education was constituted under the charge of an education officer with headquarters at Sadiya. Mrs. Indira Miri was the first Educational Officer and it was she who started the pioneering work in the field of education. Steps for implementation of Basic Education programme in NEFA started for which the teacher training institution was established in the month of December 1947 to spread the activities of the basic education programmes among the people by opening new schools. Before starting the basic training institution, twenty six teachers were trained in the Tilabar Basic Training Centre, Assam, and nine officers of the Education Department have completed Basic Training at Sevagram and Delhi.

The administration own teachers training institution which was shifted from Sadiya to Margherita during 1952 and from Margherita to Changlang in Tirap District during 1958 and re-designed as the Buniadi Shiksha Bhavan, expanded to provide training for tribal and non-tribal teachers in Basic Education. The Basic Education Training Institute was equipped to provide for a proper orientation courses of about three months duration to teachers who had qualified in Basic Education from places outside.

As stated in the beginning, the medium of instruction proved to be the most sensitive and controversial question in the whole scheme of educational development initiated by the administration. The absence of any script for most of the tribal languages complicated the issue for the administration was under obligation to introduce a script for all the languages. In other hill areas of north-east India, the Raman script had already been introduced by the Missionaries with the connivance and active support of the then British rulers.

It was originally decided that the local languages should be used as the medium of instruction even before the problem of script in which text books were to be produced was finally resolved.

This resulted in an anomalous situation. The teachers used either Hindi or Assamese depending on the background of a particular teacher and the capacity of the students to follow either language according to their training. The directive issued by the administration during 7.10.1958 read as follows :

> "Students will be taught their mother tongue, i.e. the tribal languages text books upto class III are almost ready in cyclostyled form. By the time the next session starts it is hoped to deliver the cyclostyled books upto Class V. After that the administration will be taking in hand supplementary readers and also books required for extra reading"

But the directive did not mention of the script in which the text books were written. It was, however, known that the text books in the local languages prepared. Since 1951, they were in Devanagri script.

However, the administration could not stick to the above directive long and felt that it would be rather ambitious to fix any rigid syllabus as conditions in the various blocks vary considerably.

In place where the interest of the people are motivated towards literacy teaching of Devanagiri script should be taken up. In addition, Hindi should also be taught.

The attitude reflected and partiality shown for the teaching of Hindi in the above passage, was vigorously resented by public opinion in Assam and it was a palpable proof to the people of Assam that the whole policy was a calculated attempt at alienating the tribesman from the plain people of Assam. It was argued not without apparent frustration that a broken or simplified form of Assamese language was the natural *lingua franca* in ordinary transactions and exchanges between the tribemen and the Assamese people, their next door neighbours.

In the face of mounting opposition from the Assamese public opinion, the NEFA administration obviously yielded to the pressure and decided to reverse the earlier decision on the question of medium of instruction. Henceforth, Assamese script was to be used for writing text books in local NEFA languages in place of Devanagri. By this decision, all the text books prepared since 1951 become obsolete. It was further decided after 1959 that wherever possible, Assamese should be used as medium of instruction at the middle and higher levels. In 1962 and at the end of 1965, the position with regard to medium of instruction work out as follows:

Instruction in Assamese began in grade one, Hindi in grade three and English in grade four.

With the advancement of education among several sections of the people, the controversy over the medium of instruction began taking a curious turn with tribal spokesmen taking different and often contradiction stood on the issue. The Wanchos of Tirap held demonstrations in favour of Assamese. While claiming for all Tirap students Union, T.L. Rajkumar, belonging to the Nocte tribe attributed the slow progress in the field of education to lack of proficiency of the children in the English language. The predominantly Adi students of Jawaharlal Nehru College, Pasighat (the then only college in Arunachal Pradesh established in 1964) staged demonstrations in May 1970 and again in January 1971, demanding immediate replacement of Assamese as the medium of instruction in schools, and advocating intensive teaching of Hindi and English in its place. It is not unlikely that students were influenced by the predominance of English in all other hill areas of north-east India. They were also possibly realising that knowledge of Hindi and English would help them in securing jobs in Governmental and other establishments. The attack on the education policy of the Agency, Administration also came from another direction. The emerging leadership among educated tribemen of NEFA arise vigorous objection to conversion of lower primary schools into institutions of basic education. They agreed that only formal education even at the lower stages was needed for rising the quality to the generation of NEFA's children for responsible positions in the administration and its other developmental programmes. Basic education was not going to open up doors to them in the coming decades.

In 1971 a decision was taken by the administration to affiliate all schools of NEFA to the Central School system with English as medium of instruction from upper primary onward. But this was not to the end of frequent changes of policy with regard to the medium of instruction. The second meeting of the Agency Council recommended that while pre-primary education should be imparted through local languages, primary education should be through Assamese medium and secondary education through English. According to official report, the recommendation was accepted by the Government of India along with the recommendation to align the school of NEFA to the Central School system. The upshot of this change of policy was that English was installed as the medium of instruction from Class I to Class XII.

In the meantime, a new development with future consequences was taking place in the field of education due to uneven response to the administration efforts at spreading literacy, education among the various sections of tribal population.

As a result of all these cross-current in the socio-political life of the people, a sense of separation or exclusiveness was engulfing the raising generation which had not yet found its feet, and was yet hesitant to march ahead with confidence to join the mainstream of national life. It has to be said that the sense of exclusiveness, referred to above, was often aggravated when the tribal youth from this region occasionally ventured out to distant places like New Delhi where they were looked upon as strange people from a strange land.

The deplorable ignorance of people in Delhi and far off places about the geography of the country compounded the situation, and understandably hurt their sensitivity. It was only after Chinese aggression of 1962 that the awareness of the north-east frontier of the country was momentarily generated. It is still largely a 'hidden' and 'unknown' land.

NOTES AND REFERENCES

1. P.N. Luthra, Constitutional and Administrative Growth of the North East Frontier Agency, Shillong, 1971, p. 12.
2. L.N.Chakravarty, Glimpses of the Early History of Arunachal, Shillong, 1973, p. 1.
3. Ibid, p. preface.
4. S.D.Jha, The Wealth of Arunachal Pradesh, First Edition, Delhi 1967, p. 113.
5. N.Sarkar, Buddhism Among the Mompas and Sherdukpens, Shillong, 1980.

III
DEVELOPMENT OF SCHOOL EDUCATION

Elementary Education

Before India's independence, there was no separate educational set up in NEFA (Arunachal Pradesh). There were only three schools and fifty students in 1947. It was only in 1918, the British administration opened a venture Lower Primary School at Paklek (present Pasighat, Headquarters of East Siang District), already mentioned in Chapter, 'Brief History of Arunachal Pradesh', one in 1922 another lower Primary School was established at Dambuk, now in Dibang Valley District and Sadiya was upgraded to Middle School.

Prior to that, there was no single teaching/ learning institutions in any part of Arunachal Pradesh. As the land was unknown by any Indian rulers, modern education was out of question for the people of the then NEFA. In fact, home was the only centre of learning for local children, where they were brought up and taught traditional ways of tribal life and crafts by their parents. Legends and tales were transmitted from generation to generation and this system was purely informal and verbal. Although, the Buddhist group had their own script, but was taught in the Monastry and Gompas. Their teachings were related to religion and non-Buddhist could not go for such learning. Their teaching were monastrial but no formal type of education as we are having today.

During the British period, they left the tribal people of these frontier tracts more or less to themselves. The policy of the foreign rulers had nothing to do with the spread of education in the area. Moreover, the historical circumstances and geographical factors had compelled the people to live within the confine of their hill abodes in the State of isolation and negligence. The age-old alienation had its effects on the psychology and outlook of the people. They were somewhat suspicious of outsiders and they resented their entrance into their territory. The Achigmori incident of 1953 where Tagin people killed many Indian soldiers and officials is one of the examples of such feeling. They were reluctant to accept new ideas and they clung to their own beliefs and practices.

However, with the attainment of independence in the year 1947, the new era of educational progress and development in the area started. But the problem facing the introduction of modern method of education in NEFA was a great challenge to the new administration. The people were ignorant and in the beginning were to be constantly persuaded to accept the new method and ideas of education, and students were motivated by giving some attractive articles or sweets. People were poor and their living standard was very low and unhygenic. Moreover, the interior areas were totally inaccessible and there was no question of communication. Nevertheless, the task of overcoming the initial problems and difficulties were undertaken with great zeal and a group of dedicated teachers having missionary spirit were sent to the interior places to motivate the people and to spread education. Those teachers were not only the torch-bearers of education but also the fore-runners of administration in some parts of the territory.

In the month of September 1947, the Department of Education was established under the charge of an education officer with headquarters of the Sadiya Frontier Tract, Mrs. Indira Miri was appointed as the first Education Officer. The supervision as well as the administration of the educational activities were carried on from Sadiya where a teachers training institute was established in the month of December 1947 for imparting training to the teachers and for spread of education in the interior areas. Thus spread of education in NEFA was a very tough job. Moreover, NEFA was a part of Assam and the Government of Assam and even the Union Government did not take much interest for expansion of Education in Arunachal Pradesh. It was after the Chinese Aggression in 1962 and visit of Pt. Jawaharlal Nehru in the same year, Arunachal Pradesh (NEFA) could make its existence known to the rest of the country and could create an urge in the Government of India for its overall development to bring the land and people at par with the rest of the country. It was after 1962 that the torch of the actual development was brought to NEFA in which the contributions of late D. Ering the first MP of Arunachal Pradesh should be remembered with gratitude. Moreover, there was a problem in regard to the medium of instruction in the then NEFA as people had no written script of their own. Before 1972, the medium of instruction was Assamese, Hindi to begin in Class three and English in Class four. Before that also, there were lot of controversies in this regard.

In May 1970, the students of J.N. College, Pasighat started demonstrations and again in January 1971, demanding immediate replacement of Assamese as the medium of instruction in schools and advocated for intensive teaching of Hindi and English in its place. As a result, with the attainment of the status of Union Territory and renamed as Arunachal Pradesh on January 20, 1972 English and Hindi as second language had replaced Assamese. As such, real development in education was accelerated in Arunachal Pradesh after it became a Union Territory in 1972.

As already mentioned in previous chapters, in 1947 there were only two primary schools in Arunachal Pradesh—one at Pasighat and another at Dambuk. In 1961, there were 129 primary schools against two in 1947. Particularly, during the last two decades, Arunachal Pradesh had made phenomenal progress in the field of education in general and primary education in particular. At present, in all interior most and far flung areas of the State, in every district, primary schools have been opened and free education is provided upto Class VIII standard. Now, Arunachal Pradesh has 299 pre-primary schools, 1149 primary schools and 274 Middle schools distributed in all 12 districts of the State.

The following table shows the number of Pre-Primary, Primary and Middle School, district wise.

Number of Schools - Middle, Primary and Pre-Primary - Districtwise

Sl No	Districts	Middle Schools			Primary Schools			Pre-Primary School		
		Govt	Aided un Aided	Total	Govt	Aided un Aided	Total	Govt	Aided un Aided	Total
1		2	3	4	5	6	7	8	9	10
1.	Tawang	12	-	12	51	3	54	27	-	27
2.	West Kameng	16	-	16	83	4	87	27	-	27
3.	East Kameng	19	-	19	99	2	101	19	-	19
4.	Lower Subansiri	32	-	32	105	-	105	20	-	20
5.	Upper Subansiri	23	-	23	99	1	100	16	-	16
6.	West Siang	44	-	44	146	1	147	27	-	27
7.	East Siang	29	-	29	132	1	133	40	-	40
8.	Dibang Valley	20	-	20	40	2	42	29	-	29
9.	Lohit	21	1	22	115	3	118	34	-	34
10.	Tirap	18	-	18	115	1	116	24	-	24
11.	Changlang	23	-	23	108	1	109	29	-	29
12.	Papum Pare	14	2	16	56	6	62	7	-	7
				274			1174			299

Source : Statistical Branch, DPI's Office, Naharlagun.

Growth of Elementary Schools in Arunachal Pradesh since 1961 (Middle, Primary & Pre-Primary)

Year	*No. of Elementary Schools*
1960-61	129
1965-66	314
1970-71	506
1975-76	635
1980-81	NA
1986 (September)	1199
1989-90	NA
1991-93	1448

Sources : (a) Statistical Branch, DPI's office, Naharlagun.

With the increase of educational institutions, mainly of the primary schools, Arunachal has accelerated the literacy percentage 11.03 in 1971 to 20.09 in 1981 and 32.87 according to 1991 census. Alongwith formal system of education, Adult Education Programmes, Community Education Programmes, Jana Siksha Nulayam and Non-Formal Education systems are also existing in Arunachal Pradesh through which Arunachal could increase its literacy percentage.

District-wise literacy percentage is shown in the Table below.

Districtwise Headquarters, Population and Literacy Rate—1981 - 1991 are given below.

Sl. No.	*District*	*Hqrs.*	*Population (1991)*	*Literacy 1981*	*1991*
1	East Siang	Pasighat	99,985	25.15	35.79
2	West Siang	Along	89,778	22.25	35.97
3	Lower Subansiri	Ziri	1,54,591	18.93	32.74
4	Upper Subansiri	Daporjo	49,163	12.43	29.70
5	East Kameng	Seppa	50,238	-	30.42
6	West Kameng	Bomdila	56,402	21.45	36.08
7	Tawang	Tawang	27,574	21.45	24.88
8	Dibang Valley	Anini	42,928	25.00	37.78
9	Lohit	Tezu	1,09,632	27.45	39.55
10	Tirap	Khonsa	85,210	18.70	24.38
11	Changlang	Changlang	92,891	18.70	33.42
	Total		8,58,392	20.09	32.87

Sources : (a) 1981 Census report, Govt. of India.
(b) 1991 Census - Manorama Year Book (1990 & 1992)

The State Government is giving special attention to elementary education for its rapid development and progress. Not only free education is being imparted but it is also providing the students mid-day meals, school uniforms, books, etc. for which the government is spending large amount every year. For Mid-day Meals, Rs. 2,68,93,27 was sanctioned during the session 1991-92 and that amount is still being used. For uniforms, during 1991-92, Rs. 1,07,24,185 was sanctioned and during 1992-93, Rs. 1,28,52,145 was sanctioned and utilized for the purpose. Various other facilities are also provided in the primary schools to motivate the students such as sports goods, science kits, library books, etc. Primary school teachers are also given special training at DIET, Changlang.

Alongwith the increase of elementary education, the number of other educational institutions have also been increased rapidly and enrolment at various stages have also been increased. Number of various types of institutions, number of enrolment by department as on 31.3.93, and number of Scheduled Tribe students by department as on 31.3.93 are given in Table below, district-wise.

Growth of Elementary Schools and Enrolment

Year	*No. of Elementary Schools*	*Enrolments*		
		Boys	*Girls*	*Total*
1960-61	129	NA	NA	4201
1965-66	314	NA	NA	10404
1970-71	506	14751	4168	18919
1975-76	635	NA	NA	36344
1980-81	NA	39775	20129	48835
1986-88	1199	52519	35504	88023
1989-90	NA	62007	45126	107133
1991-93	1448	90078	64185	154263

Enrolment of Secondary and Higher Secondary Levels of Education

Year	*Secondary level (Class IX - X) Enrolment*			*Higher Sec. Level (Class XI - XII) Enrolment*		
	Boys	*Girls*	*Total*	*Boys*	*Girls*	*Total*
1976-77	736	185	921	335	49	384
1981-82	2426	927	3353	1303	323	1626
1986-87	5213	2239	7452	1918	662	2580
1988-89	6091	2762	8853	2610	856	3466
1990-93	8104	4704	12808	4325	1652	5977

Source : (a) Statistical Branch, DPI's Office, Naharlagun.
(b) A Study of Teachers Education Programmes in Arunachal Pradesh, Kamduk, Duly.

Educational Organization and Administrative Structure

Since education is the State subject, the organisation and structure of education are largely concern of the State. Each State independently determines the educational structure to be adopted, particularly at the school stage. Some variations may be found in the educational structure within the school stage. The Primary and Middle stages together constitute the elementary stage. In Arunachal Pradesh, we have 5 years of primary schooling, 3 years of Middle and two years of secondary schooling pattern. In many States still, the first ten years of schooling is divided into 4 years of primary, three years of upper primary and three years of secondary schooling. However, the common pattern of 5+3+2 has been suggested to all States by 1995 in the NPE, 1986. Then, in Higher Secondary and college level, like that of the other States of India, Arunachal follows CBSE pattern of 10+2+3.

After completing 10 years of general education, a student may opt science or humanities stream or commerce or vocational course, but in Arunachal Pradesh, all Higher Secondary Schools do not have vocational and commerce stream after completion of higher secondary

Secondary and Higher Secondary Education

In 1947, there was no Secondary and Higher schools, except two primary schools at Pasighat and Dambuk. After independence, 1948, Middle School at Pasighat was upgraded to High School. Development of Secondary and Higher Secondary Schools had been very slow in Arunachal Pradesh. In 1961, there were 5 High Schools and 4 full-fledged Higher Secondary Schools and all these schools were affiliated to the Board of Secondary Education,Assam. Each High School was equipped with science laboratories, library and sports equipments. Students were provided with hostel facilities, stipends and free text books. Science is compulsory in all High Schools of Arunachal Pradesh, General Science at Middle school stage and Environmental Study at primary level. In all higher secondary schools, there are two streams - Science and Humanities. Of course, many schools are having no Science stream due to paucity of fund from the Education Department. Commerce stream have also been opened in some of the schools - Bomdila, Doimukh and Pasighat. Vocational course have also been introduced in 4 Higher Secondary schools - Basar, Bomdila, Doimukh and Pasighat. In Arunachal Pradesh, secondary and higher secondary schools are following the CBSC pattern — 10+2+3 pattern of education.

As already mentioned, the progress of Secondary and Higher Secondary schools had been very slow. However, during the last decade, especially 1980s, Arunachal Pradesh has made a tremendous progress in this direction. Now, Arunachal Pradesh has 84 Secondary Schools and 55 Higher Secondary Schools, distributed in 12 districts of the State. In the table given below, number of Secondary and Higher Secondary Schools, district wise, is shown:

Districtwise Number of Secondary and Higher Secondary Schools in Arunachal Pradesh

Sl No	*Districts*	*Higher Secondary Schools*				*Secondary Schools*			
		Govt	*Local Bodies*	*Aided Unaided*	*Total*	*Govt*	*Local Bodies*	*Aided Unaided*	*Total*
1.	Tawang	1	-	-	1	3	-	-	3
2.	West Kameng	3	-	-	3	8	-	-	8
3.	East Kameng	2	-	-	2	5	-	-	5
4.	Lower Subansiri	5	1	-	6	6	-	-	6
5.	Upper Subansiri	2	-	-	2	6	-	-	6
6.	West Siang	7	1	-	8	10	-	-	10
7.	East Siang	10	-	-	10	8	-	1	9
8.	Dibang Valley	4	-	-	4	5	-	-	5
9.	Lohit	5	-	-	5	11	-	1	12
10.	Tirap	3	2	-	5	6	-	-	6
11.	Changlang	4	-	-	4	9	-	1	10
12.	Papum Pare	5	-	-	5	3	-	1	4
	Total	51	4	-	55	80	-	4	84

Source : Statistical Branch, DPI's Office, Naharlagun.

Besides Government Secondary and Higher Secondary Schools in Arunachal Pradesh, National Open School centres have been opened at four Higher Secondary Schools of Arunachal Pradesh to impart education at these two levels for those who are unable to continue their education in the formal or Government Schools. Class V passed candidate may directly take admission in Class VIII. Eighth passed may take addmission in Class X and tenth passed candidate may take admission in Class XII. The certificates of NOS is equally recognised like that of CBSE passed certificate. Basically it is job oriented examination. These four open school centres are run in Government Higher Secondary Schools, Itanagar, Bomdila, Pasighat and Kendriya Vidyalaya, Itanagar. At Pasighat, since 1990-91, 57 candidates have qualified Class XII and 78 candidates qualified Class X so far i.e. till 1992-93.

Higher Secondary and Secondary Schools Managed by other Agencies

	Schools	*District*
	Higher Secondary	
1.	Kendriya Vidyalaya No. I, Naharlagun	Papum Pare
2.	Donyi-Polo Vidya Bhavan, Itanagar	Papum Pare
3.	Kendriya Vidyalaya, Tenga Valley	West Kameng
4.	R.K. Mission, Along	West Siang
5.	R.K. Mission, Narottam Nagar, Depmali	Tirap
6.	R.K. Sarada Mission, Khonsa	Tirap
7.	Jawahar Navodaya Vidyalaya, Roing	Dibang valley
8.	Jawahar Navodaya Vidyalaya, Tissa	Tirap
9.	Jawahar Navodaya Vidyalaya, Lepariang	U/Subansiri
10.	Jawahar Navodaya Vidyalaya, Seppa	E/Kameng
11.	Jawahar Navodaya Vidyalaya, Mahadevpur	Lohit
	Secondary Schools	
1.	Kendriya Vidyalaya No. II, Itanagar	Papum Pare
2.	Prantiya Samaj Kalyan Ashram, Kimin	Papum Pare
3.	Baum Kakir Mission, Boleng	East Siang
4.	Kendriya Vidyalaya, Pasighat	East Siang
5.	V.K.V. School, Jairampur	Changlang
6.	Kendriya Vidyalaya, Rupa	West Kameng
7.	V.K.V. School, Tafromgam (Girls)	Lohit
8.	Kendriya Vidyalaya, Tezu	Lohit

Development of School Education: A Trend Analysis

Since the territory was hidden to the people of India during the ancient and medieval period, the system of formal education in particular had been conspicuously absent in the past in Arunachal Pradesh. The history of education in Arunachal Pradesh reveals that the North-West portion of the Kameng district, the mythological education used to be imparted through Buddhist Monastry; otherwise the formal system of education was introduced by the Adis during the British period. The first ventured school was opened by the local people at Pasighat in 1918. The Adis of Dibang Valley also opened a similar school at Damuk in 1922. The medium of teaching in both the schools was Assamese. After passing out Class III standard, the students of these schools had to go to Sadiya Middle English School named by the American Baptist Mission for further studies.

Arunachal Pradesh made a humble beginning in the field of educational growth only when NEFA was carved out of Assam with its headquarters at Shillong. The real development in education was accelerated in Arunachal Pradesh when she was made a Union Territory in 1972. In the same year the medium of education in Arunachal Pradesh became English instead of Assamese, and school education comes under CBSE course, Delhi. It was under Assam Education Board till 1972. When the administration of the vast hilly territory of Arunachal Pradesh was taken over by our own government in 1947, it was an uphill task to take up any developmental activities in the area mainly because of non-availability of proper communication facilities and the aged traditions and customs of the people. In this task the basic policy followed by the government is to approach tribal life and culture with respect and affection and to introduce the good things of modern life in a gentle and persuasive way. The people have themselves felt the benefit of the various projects for the development of education, agriculture, health, communication, cottage industry, etc.

Despite difficult terrain, communication problems and lack of other resources, significant progress has been made during this period. Education played its vital role in the development process. There were only two primary schools in Arunachal Pradesh (then NEFA) in 1947. But now the Educational Network during the first decade of political independence, that till 1957-58, the number of educational institutions rose to 105. The first census conducted in the human population of Arunachal Pradesh during 1961 reveals that there were 3,36,558 population and about 148 educational institutions with the total enrolment of 4,443. In the year 1973, the educational institution rose up to 567 with the total enrolment of 33,000. The territory reached the literacy rate of 11.29 in 1971. From a nil base the percentage of literacy in Arunachal Pradesh has attained the figure of 20.09 at the time of (3rd census in Arunachal) 1981 census. The significant progress can be observed in this period. The number of educational institute rose up to 1,039 with the total number of students of 67,363. From these figures it may be observed that the percentage growth rate of enrolment is credibly higher than the same growth of the educational institutions during the corresponding years. There are 3257 habitations in the state out of which 1778 are having primary schools and 1479 habitations are without primary schools. Out of 1479 habitations 1150 habitations are below 100 population slab and 110 are 200 or more population slab where primary or L.V. are being opened during 1989-90, since there are 1150 habitations below 100 population slab without facility for primary education situated in the remote interior areas where it is not feasible to open primary school with hardly 10 children available for primary education. On experimental basis one community school has been taken in one of such locations with provision of a regualr teacher for providing formal school education to the children and also Non-Formal Education and Adult Education. Remarkable progress has been achieved in the field of education. The census report 1991 reveals that there are 8,58,392 population in the state. The literacy rate is 32.87 (Male 41.30% and Female 23.03%). There are 284 Pre-primary schools, 1144 Primary Schools, 73 Secondary Schools, 48 Higher Secondary Schools. Thus it reveals that now Arunachal Pradesh possesses about 1823 Educational Institutions with the total enrolment of more than 1,61,000 students and more than six thousand teaching staff.

Arunachal has seen tremendous expansion of school educational facilities since 1947. The state is not lagging much behind in comparison to other North-Eastern States where school education started long before the independence. If we examine the following table, we will be able to see the quantitative expansion of school education in North-Eastern States and the position of Arunachal Pradesh.

State	*No. of Primary school*	*No. of Upper primary school*	*No. of Secondary school school*	*No of Higher Secondary*
Arunachal Pradesh	952	182	73	48
Assam	25,873	4991	2330	365
Manipur	2,630	436	336	10
Meghalaya	3,683	665	288	2
Mizoram	1,004	463	160	-
Nagaland	1,131	291	95	-
Tripura	1,927	419	280	100

Critical Review of School Education:

The state has been trying to provide universal primary education keeping in mind the basic education is most important to raise the literacy rate in the area. Although the number of schools have been increasing very fast but there are some areas, the number of school going students is increasing day by day and the existing schools are not able to provide prospectives with enough accommodation as they are full to capacity (Payeng, 1988).

The National Council of Applied Economic Research (NCAER) Report (1967) has dealtwith Education in the state (then NEFA) in great details and has been very critical of it. Commenting on the basic education in primary and middle school levels, the Council feels that basic education in Schools as it is being imported at present does not meet the needs of situation. It also observed that the present frame work of the secondary and higher education in the state (then NEFA) is based on wrong assumption. The report says that purely general education will lead NEFA not far, for the employment potential for the educated youngmen is getting lower and lower every year. The council cautions against the dangers of liberal education and has suggested diversification right from middle school level (Ering, 1972). In the primary stage, while efforts will be directed towards teaching the 3 R's accent will be on elementary agriculture and training in handling the tools for some of the generally useful crafts, such as carpentry and smithy. At the middle level, the main emphasis will be on agriculture but students who show promise in any non-agricultural craft could be given more advanced courses and prepared for further technical schools. At Higher Secondary stage, the weeding out process having been completed, full emphasis will be given on the general academic education, side by side with such a pattern, there should be well run demonstration farms at central place where those students who are weeded out at the secondary school stage can go through a regular course for a year or two. This would mean a complete orientation of the system of education. The whole education system may be so oriented that by the middle school stage it should be possible to separately identify the mainstream of students. One stream would consist of those students who receive further general education in high schools (of which the best may go into university education), while another stream would go in for further training in farming techniques and another for craft training. These streams would thin out considerably after the high school stage, only the more promising going on for graduate studies.

There is a good deal of truth what the NCAER has said about the problem of education in NEFA. The policy or programme of education needs to be amended and tailored to the needs.

The very important lapse in the school education is that there is no curriculum cell or school education board of its own. As the schools are affiliated the CBSE, New Delhi, students are to study enrolled in the school neither understand any language or any alphabet. It is very difficult for the teacher as well as for the learners to communicate without local language or dialect. Wereas the autonomous hill district of Assam, their respective mother-tongue constitute the medium of instruction for primary education. In Nagaland also, the respective tribal languages are their medium of instruction at the primary stage. Ao and Angami languages are taught in the secondary stage, also Khasi as a language subject up to the post-graduate standard in Guwahati University and NEHU. In Manipur a number of books have been published in different languages. Until 1965, the policy followed by the NEFA Administration was to prepare special text-books for the primary schools in the tribal dialects of the area. A large number of books were prepared and printed in the Devnagari script. After the primary school stage where medium of instruction was Assamese, Hindi was introduced. In some schools, Hindi was the medium of instruction from that stage onwards. English was introduced in Class V.

After 1965, the policy has been substantially modified, on the recommendation of a committee headed by D.Ering, Deputy Minister of the Union Government who hails from Arunachal Pradesh. The representatives of the local people wanted that either Hindi or English should be introduced as the medium of instruction at the earliest stage. In most of the areas the Administration has discontinued the teaching of the text-books prepared in the various tribal languages.

It is not clear whether the Ering Committee had the benefit of consultation with educationists who have experiences of scientific research in such matters. In a report on the medium of instruction, published by UNESCO, it has been recommended that even in those cases where leaders of the local people do not want their language to be the medium of instruction in the beginners class, an attempt should be made to persuade them to change their mind. It is based on sound pedagogical principles. Sometimes it happens that in the first stage of acculturation, the people concerned develop an inferiority complex about their own culture. They try to discard what they have and imitate cultures of the advanced communities. But at a second stage, there is a re-assertion of self-respect which leads to selective revival of the past. But in the feeling of being cheated by the donor group, the language policy in NEFA should be reexamined keeping this also in view. Of course the state government has made every effort to improve the school education by sending the representatives in the curriculum process and planning. The text books have been revised in the light of the local content. In addition to that the state govt. has established a Tribal Dialect Development Centre in the Arunachal University which has prepared the text book in local dialect for the beginners in primary education in some of the dialect and those books will be introduced in the schools very soon. Further the Govt. has introduced the vocational Education in the school system very recently. It is also expected that integrated approach will be made for qualitative improvement of the school education in the state which will cater the needs of the people in the state.

References

1. Bhattacharjee, J.B. (ed) : Sequences in Development in North East India, Omsons Publications, New Delhi, 1989.
2. Census of India 1971.
3. Census of India 1981.
4. Census of India 1991.
5. Faure, Edgar (Ed) : Learning to Be, UNESCO, Paris, 1972.
6. Biswas, N.B. Educational Anthropology in Arunachal Pradesh: Prospects for School Curriculum, RESARUN, journal of the Department of Research, Vol, XVIII No. 1 and 2, Itanagar, 1992.
7. Ering, D. The North East Frontier Agency in the Tribal Situation in India, IIAS, Shimla, 1972.

IV
HIGHER EDUCATION

Genesis of Higher Education in Arunachal Pradesh

The term "higher education" should be used in a very clearcut way. There is a possible broad sense of the word with a meaning close to that of post secondary education. In a restricted sense, higher education refers only to universities, and prestigious professional schools or artistic training. "Encyclopaedia of Britannica" has refered higher education, as, "any or various types of education given in post secondary institutions of learning and usually affording, at the end of a course of study, a named degree or certificate. The institution includes not only universities and colleges but also various professional schools that provide preparation in such fields as law, theology, medicine, music and art and, in addition separately organised teacher-training schools, Junior colleges and various kinds of institutes of technology" (Encyclopaedia of Britannica, Vol. V, P-917). The best short definition of higher education may be the one devised and accepted in 1962 by 44 nations participating in a UNESCO conference on higher education in Africa.

Higher education is defined as all types of education (academic, professional, technological, or teacher education) provided in institutions such as universities, liberal arts colleges for which: (a) the basic entrance requirement is completion of secondary education ......, (b) the usual entrance age is about 18 years ; and (c) in which the courses lead to the giving of a named award (degree, diploma, or certificate of higher studies—Encyclopaedia of Britannica, Vol-18, P.- 1).

The present study is carried out keeping in view the above definition of higher education. The discussion starts with the beginning of the higher education that is colleges, followed by university, teacher training, technical education, medical, law colleges, etc. along with their organisation and structure, curriculum, examinations, etc. The higher education system has important responsibilities to the society as a whole, as well as, to the educational system itself. The significance of the traditional functions of acquisition, preservation, dissemination and extension of the frontier of knowledge, the balanced education of individuals and the training of higher level personnel for all walks of life is obvious. But higher education in Arunachal Pradesh has to undertake special care to the needs and aspirations of the tribal people of the state, with a view to develop the intellectual, academic and cultural advancement of the people.

Arunachal could boast of rapid development in the sphere of school education even in the early part of sixtees, while it was peeping into the stream light of civilization but it did not have a single institution of higher learning. The college going students had to go to distant places for higher education in those days. Dr. Daying Ering, the pioneer leader in the field of education of the land, realised the problem. He had a vision to have a college in the then NEFA to cater to the needs of higher education. Dr. Daying Ering, the hero of the land when became the Member of the Parliament took up the issue of establishment of a college on behalf of the people. Ultimately it was agreed at higher level. The government was ready to translate the aspirations of the people into action. Thus, the premier institution of higher learning in Arunachal Pradesh was established in the month of July, 1964, on the bank of the mighty and vivacious Siang. The college is named after Pt. Jawaharlal Nehru. The college started functioning with 42 students and eight lecturers at Pasighat. It offered pre-university course in English, Assamese, Economics, Geography, History, Political science, Hindi and Education. Honours courses in English, Political science and History were introduced in 1965. Honours course in Geography was introduced in 1978. The said courses in Economics and Hindi also started in 1975 and 1987 respectively. Pre-university science classes in Physics, Chemistry, Botany, Zoology and Mathematics started functioning in 1973. In 1976 all these subjects were introduced in degree class and honours courses in all these science subjects were offered to the students in 1978. Although commerce was taught as a subject from the session 1965-66, but honours course in commerce was introduced during 1989-90 session. The Post Graduate section in History and Political science was opened in 1981 and the college was upgraded to a P.G. College. Thus, it reveals that Jawaharlal Nehru College was the only educational centre in the state imparting higher education to the young boys and girls of Arunachal Pradesh. It was the only clearing house of Arunachal in catering to the requirements of efficient manpower in the state. Keeping pace with development in all spheres of course, one more college was established in 1979 at Itanagar. J.N.College, Pasighat and Govt. College, Itanagar were affiliated to Guwahati University since their inception. Accordingly it had to and they followed the Ordinances of the Guwahati University so far academic exercises were concerned (Admission, Curriculum, Examination, etc.). In addition to the affinity, Guwahati University was the nearest institution for convenience in all respects. But a lot of inconvenience and dislocation was caused in the normal functioning of these colleges, due to continuing agitation in Assam. Consequently, the Govt. of Arunachal Pradesh approached the Govt. of India to get these colleges affiliated to any other university, having such status for extra territorial affiliation. After much efforts, these colleges were affiliated to the Punjab University (Chandigarh) in 1980.

Having affiliated the colleges to the Punjab University, problems of higher education were not solved. The different types of problems cropped up like the duration of the first degree courses, the block period prescribed by Punjab University for the students graduating from Guwahati University for admission to the post graduate courses, conductance of examinations, etc. came in the way of the students in getting the higher education. The people of Arunachal tried their best to find out the solution of the problem forever. They have been trying to establish a university of their own in the territory. There was demand from the public to the Hon'ble Chief Minister for the same. The Chief Minister after discussing the matter with University Grants Commission (UGC), wrote a letter to the then Prime Minister Mrs. Indira Gandhi for accepting the proposal to set up a university in principle. Thereafter, a committee was appointed by the Govt. of India (Ministry of Education/University Grants Commission), to make recommendations regarding the strategy of development of higher education in Arunachal Pradesh. The committee finally recommended the establishment of a university in the territory. In accordance with recommendation, the Draft University Bill, 1983, was prepared by the Committee of Govt. of India. In the wake of, it was approved by the Centre. Finally, the Arunachal Pradesh University Bill, 1983, was moved by the Chief Minister on 10th session of the Second Legislative Assembly of Arunachal Pradesh on 3rd February, 1984. Thus, the Arunachal University Act, 1984 came on vogue. On 4th February, 1984, the then Prime Minister Mrs. Indira Gandhi laid the foundation stone of the Arunachal University at Rono hills near Doimukh on 302 acres of land. The university was virtually set up on 1st April, 1985 and the teaching commenced from that time onwards.

Organization of Higher Education

As per Arunachal University Act 1984, the purpose of the university is "to establish and incorporate a teaching and affiliating university for the Union Territory (now state) of Arunachal Pradesh." The object of the university is to disseminate and advance knowledge by providing instructional and research facilities in such branches of learning as it may deem fit, and endeavour through research, education, training and extension to play a positive role in the socio-economic and cultural development of Arunachal Pradesh based on the rich heritage of its people. Towards this it shall undertake -

(i) to strengthen and diversify certificate and diploma courses related to the needs of employment, and building the economy of the region on the basis of its natural resources;

(ii) to introduce relevant undergraduate courses for enhancing knowledge and skills;

(iii) to provide education and training in the various arts, crafts and skills of the region, raising their quality, and improving their availability to the people;

(iv) to provide or arrange training of teachers required for such activities or institutions;

(v) to provide training and other facilities to equip persons for different categories of jobs;

(vi) to provide suitable postgraduate courses of study;

(vii) to undertake and organise research to develop the creative potential of its people for optimal use of the resources of the territory particularly that which is related to regional development; and

(viii) to provide for counselling and guidance and facilities for helping in placement of students.

Immediately after commencement of the University Act, the colleges at Pasighat and Itanagar which were then affiliated to the Punjub University came under the jurisdiction of the Arunachal University for B.A./B.Com./B.Sc. (degree course) and for M.A. courses.

An Acacemic Advisory Committee was constituted to go into details and scrutinise draft regulations and ordinances required for getting admission and outline the courses at the undergraduate level. The Academic Advisory Committee held its deliberations at Itanagar on 3rd and 4th june, 1986 and submitted its recommendations to the University with national system of education, 10+2+3 pattern be followed in Arunachal University and students after passing 10+2 (Higher Secondary Examination) be admitted to 2 year B.A./B.Sc./ B.Com. pass courses, the students after passing the pass course if otherwise will be admitted to one-year Honours course.

One year Pre-University course abolished and students who failed in Pre-University examination conducted in April, 1986 were given two chances, one in September and another in April, 1987 to clear the examination.

During the session 1986-87, a college by the name of Indira Gandhi Govt. College was started at Tezu on a plot of 200 acres of land. The college was granted affiliation for undergraduate studies in English, Hindi, History, Political Science and Economics.

One more new college was started during the session 1988-89 at Bomdila, the District Headquarter of West Kameng District. The college was granted affiliation for undergraduate studies in English, Economics, History, Geography, Political Science and Hindi.

The growth and development of higher education in Arunachal can be examined from the following table:

Enrolment in Higher Education

	1985-86	*1986-87*	*1987-88*	*1988-89*	*1989-90*	*1990-91*
Pre-university	107	22	Exam April,88	-		
B.A.	839	1023	1044	1087 H=160	1034 H=307	1209 H=328
B.Sc.	58	58	53	69 H=13	34 H=19	34 H=20
B.Com.	27	37	29	37	57 H=10	98 H=10
M.A.Pol.Science	14	15	48	21	19	34
M.A. History.	23	22	58	38	13	15
M.A. Economics.	-	-	-	-	-	-
M.A. English.	-	-	-	-	-	02
M.A. Geography.	-	-	-	-	-	
B.Ed.	-	-	-	16	25	23
M.Ed.	-	-	-	-	03	05

The Court, the Executive Council, The Planning Board, the Academic Council, (Faculties and Board of Studies) are the statutory bodies through which the administration of the university is organised.

Access in Higher Education

The access to higher education covers the criteria and requirements for gaining admission to higher education. In some places people enter into higher education without completing secondary school. For the purposes of this paper, higher education in Arunachal simply refers to education offered by post-secondary institutions. In Arunachal Pradesh access to higher education refers criteria or eligibility for admission in the colleges or in the university after completing secondary/higher secondary courses.

Criteria and Procedures for Access to Undergraduate Course

The eligibility for the courses leading to the Bachelor of Arts (B.A.), Bachelor of Science (B.Sc.) and Bachelor of Commerce (B.Com) at the pass and honours levels are as follows :

Students who have passed the Higher Secondary Examination conducted by the CBSE or any other equivalent examination from any other recognised Board/University are eligible to seek admission to the first year of the Degree Course. The duration of the degree courses, both pass and Honours are three years.

Procedure and Criteria for Access to the Master Degree Programmes in Arts, Science and Commerce

The master degree programme is spread over a period of two academic years. The programme will not be combined with any other course offered by the university except those which may be designed by the university specially for the post-graduate students of the university.

Admission to the programme is made only at the beginning of each academic year unless specifically decided for a course by the Academic Council. The candidates who have taken the Bachelor Degree (Pass & Honours) of the Arunachal University or any other recognised university shall be eligible to apply for admission subject provisions of the regulations relating to pre-requisites, if any. The minimum qualifying marks for admission is 45% provided that a relaxation of 5% marks may be given to the Scheduled Tribes Scheduled Caste candidates.

Curriculum in Higher Education

The term "curriculum" refers to the structure as well as the content of education. To develop the curriculum systematically is to analyse and state educational objectives clearly, and to shape the content of courses, the patterns of programmes, the methods of teaching and learning, and the modes of assessment into forms consistent with these overall goals (International Ency. of Education, P - 2196).

In higher education, the degree of standardization of courses varies according to disciplines, types of institutions and historical traditions of the country.

The curriculum development in higher education in Arunachal Pradesh starts with the establishment of the Arunachal University. The university in the initial year of its existence (1986) adopted the same course of studies and syllabi as prescribed by the Punjab University for the session 1986-87. One year Pre-University course was abolished in order to switch over to 10+2+3 system. Candidates who have passed Pre-University were admitted into B.A. in the Govt. College, Itanagar, which was considered as equivalent to class XII examination directly to B.A./B.Sc./B.Com Part II to continue with two year pass degree course based on the syllabi as prescribed by the Punjab University to which the colleges were affiliated till the development of the curriculum by the Arunachal University. In term of the national pattern of education most universities in the country have switched over to the three-year degree pattern. To cope with national pattern of education the Arunachal University had taken the following measures :

The two year degree course has been extended to the third year Honours course from the academic session started on 1st July, 1988. The structure for the honours courses for B.A./B.Sc./B.Com programme was approved by the Arunachal University Committee as recommended by the Academic Advisory Committee. The course outline in respect of these were got finalised with help of the subject committees in each subject. During the session 1987-88, steps were taken for the preparation of three-year degree course (Pass and Honours) for Arts/Science/Commerce. In accordance with the Ordinances, Faculties and Board of Studies were constituted. Detailed syllabi were drawn up for the three-year degree programme starting from 1988. In addition, detailed syllabi for Master Degree programme in History, Political Science, Education, English, Economics, Geography Tribal studies, Commerce, Zoology and Botany were also finalised and are in vogue.

At present the curriculum and syllabi for the graduation and post-graduation are implemented throughout the state. English and Foundation courses are compulsory in the graduation programme. Arunachal University offers the following elective subjects in B.A./B.Sc./B.Com courses - English, Hindi, Assamese, Political Science, History, Economics, Education, Geography, Physics, Chemistry, Botany, Zoology, Mathematics and all the branches of Commerce. The course structure in three-year degree programme is furnished below:

Structure: Bachelor of Arts, Science and Commerce (Pass and Honours) Courses

There shall be a common programme of study in the first year at the end of which there shall be a university examination. Students securing 45% marks in a subject may be allowed to join the honours programme in the subject. However, there will be relaxation of 5% marks in the case of Scheduled tribe & Scheduled caste students. There will be a university examination at the end of the second and third years for both Pass and Honours students.

A) Bachelor of Arts (B.A.) Pass and Honours

The B.A. pass candidate shall study English, the Foundation Course and two elective subjects. The Honours student shall study the same course as in the English and one elective subsidiary courses in the Honours subject.

BA Pass and Honours Course Stucture

	B.A. Pass			B.A. Honours		
Year	*Subject*	*No of Papers*	*Marks*	*Subject*	*No. of Papers*	*Marks*
First	English	1	100	English	1	100
	Foundation Course	1	100	Foundation Course	1	100
	Two Elective	2x1	200	Two Elective	2x1	200
Second	English	2	200	English	1	100
	Two Elective	2x1	200	Elective Subsidiary	1	100
				Elective Honours	3	300
Third	Elective	2x2	400	Elective Honours	5	500

B) Bachelor of Science (B.SC.) Pass & Honours

The B.Sc. pass candidate shall study English, The Foundation course and three elective subjects in the first year. The Honours student shall study the same course as two elective subsidiary subjects besides courses in the Honours subjects.

B.Sc. Pass and Honours Course Structure

	B.Sc. Pass			B.Sc. Honours		
Year	*Subject*	*No of Papers*	*Marks*	*Subject*	*No. of Papers*	*Marks*
First	English	1	100	English	1	100
	Foundation Course	1	100	Foundation Course	1	100
	Elective	3x1	300	Elective	3x1	300
Second	3 Electives			Electives		
	1st	1	100	i) Subsidiary subjects	2x1	200
	2nd	2	200	(ii) Honours subjects	3	300
	3rd	2	200			
Third	3 Electives			Elective		
	1st	2	200	Hon. subjects	5	500
	2nd	1	100			
	3rd	1	100			

C) Bachelor of Commerce (B.Com.) Pass & Honours

The B.Com pass student shall study English, The Foundation Course and three elective subjects in the first year. The Honours student will study the same course as in the Pass course in the first year and thereafter additional courses.

B.Com Pass and Honours Course Structure

	B.Com. Pass			B.Com. Honours		
Year	*Subject*	*No of Papers*	*Marks*	*Subject*	*No. of Papers*	*Marks*
First	English	1	100	English	1	100
	Foundation Course	1	100	Foundation Course	1	100
	Elective	3xl	300	Elective	3xl	300
Second	Commercial Geography	1	100	Mathematics	1	100
	Commercial Law	1	100	Commercial Law	1	100
	Electives	3xl	300	Hon. Sub. group	1x2	200
Third	Company Law & Secretarial practice	1	100	Company Law & Secretarial Practice	1	100
	Income Tax & Auditing	1	100	Income Tax & Auditing	1	100
	Electives	3xl	300	Electives Honours Subject group	1x2	200

The Courses of Study (B.Ed.)

	Paper	*Written Examination*	*Sessional Work*	*Total Marks*
1.	Teacher & Society	80	20	100
2.	Educational Psychology	80	20	100
3.	Education Technology	80	20	100
4.	Problems of Education in India with special reference to North East region.	80	20	100
5&6	Special courses (Any two*)	40	10	50
7 & 8	Teaching specialization (Any two**)	80	20	100

*** Special courses will include :**

(1) Adult Education
(2) Education and Rural Education
(3) Special Education for the Gifted and the Backward.
(4) Educational Guidance & Counselling.
(5) Educational Management.
(6) Population Education.

**** Teaching Specialisation Courses include :**

(a) History
(b) Geography
(c) English/Hindi
(d) Mathematics
(e) Life Sciences
(f) Physical Sciences

Written examination of courses carrying 80 marks will be of three hours duration and those carrying 40 marks of 2 hours duration to be conducted by the university. Sessional work will be assessed internally by the department.

The Course of Study — **B.Ed.**

— **M.Ed.**

The course will consist of three core papers (EC : 1, EC : 2, and EC : 3) and two optional papers. One of the optional papers (EC : 4) will be selected from the Optional Group 'A' and the other optional paper (EC : 5) from the Optional Group 'B'. The dissertation work is compulsory for all students. The marks in each core and optional papers (EC : 1 to EC : 5) shall be one hundred out of which 20 marks are kept for sessional work. The dissertation carries 100 marks. The detailed course structure along with the weightage of marks is as follows:

Course No.	*Paper*	*Written Examination*	*Sessional Work*	*Total Marks*
EC : 1	Philosophy and Sociology of Education	80	20	100
EC : 2	Advanced Educational Psychology	80	20	100
EC : 3	Methodology of Research in Education	80	20	100
EC : 4	Option I (Any one paper from Group 'A')	80	20	100
EC : 5	Option II (Any one paper from Group 'B')	80	20	100
	Dissertation	-	-	100

Optional Group 'A'

1. Educational Technology
2. Early Childhood Education
3. Population Education
4. History of Education
5. Education of Children with Special Needs
6. Educational Measurement and Evaluation
7. Non-Formal and Adult Education
8. Curriculum Development and Evaluation
9. Programmes in Teacher Education

Optional Group 'B'

1. Distance Education
2. Guidance and Counselling
3. Environmental Education
4. Comparative Education
5. Education of Tribal Children
6. Advanced Educational Statistics
7. Education for Rural Development
8. Educational Planning and Finance
9. Trends and Issues in Teacher education

Evaluation System in Higher Education

In developing country like us there has been some interest in continuous assessment and objective testing but for the most parts of the universities traditional methods predominate. "If we wish to discover the truth about an educational system we must look into its assessment procedure" (Rowntree, 1977). Although there is sympathy for forms of assessment such as essays, projects, and specially dissertations which can foster intrinsic motivation and a commitment of learning, these methods are difficult to develop where there are poor infrastructural facilities. Arunachal University is not an exception. The state is only at the take off stage in the field of higher education. Formally during the last eight years, the state has evolved its own higher education system.

We have seen that the Arunachal University on its coming into existence adopted the same course of syllabi and subjects of teaching as prescribed by the Punjab University for the session 1985-86, for its affiliated colleges viz. Jawaharlal Nehru College, Pasighat and Govt. College, Itanagar. The students enrolled in these two colleges and having registration with the Punjab University were registered under the Arunachal University during 1985-86 session. Arunachal University followed the traditional system of evaluation through annual examination. The university conducted examinations for the first time for under-graduate as well as post-graduate students in 1986. University Examinations were conducted in two sessions—one in April and the other in September (supplementary examinations). Assistance of Punjab University has been taken in setting question papers and evaluating answer script at the initial years (during the transition period). The next session examinations were conducted in April, 1987. The annual examination for the session 1987-88 were conducted in April 88. The annual examination for the session 1988-89 were conducted in April/May, 1989. So far the examination is concerned Arunachal University had to cover both the two year Degree Course with the one-year extended Honours Course introduced by this university and the university's intergrated Three-year Degree Course. During the transition period of higher education in Arunachal Pradesh, the Arunachal University had to conduct supplementary/

compartmental examinations under Punjab University system in September 1989. Initially, there was no supplementary/compartmental system in the Three-year Degree Course. The first compartmental examination under this system was conducted in April/May, 1990 and supplementary in September/October, 1990. The two-year Degree Course under Punjab University system ceased in 1990. The one year extended Honours Course was continued up to 1990-91 Session.

The annual examination of B.A./B.Sc./B.Com./B.Ed./M.A. (Previous and Final) and M.Ed. together with compartmental examinations under Punjab University system were conducted during April/May, 1991. The new Three-year Degree Course relating to Pass and Honours of B.A./B.Sc./B.Com annual examination was conducted first during April/May, 1992. The newly introduced M.A. (Previous) and M.A. (Final) became effective from the session 1989-90. The first examination of M.A. (Previous) was conducted during 1989-90. The second M.A. (Previous) and first M.A. (Fail) was conducted in 1991. The first B.Ed. examination was conducted in 1989 and first M.Ed. was introduced in 1989 and first M.Ed. examination was conducted in 1990.

The university has evolved its own strategy for conducting the examination. The question papers are set by the teachers from other universities and evaluation or answer scripts are also done by the teachers of other universities. No internal assessment is made in any examinations except in B.Ed. and M.Ed. examinations. The evaluation scheme in various programmes are as follows :

The Arunachal University conducted examination annually for all the programmes i.e. Bachelor of Arts, Science, Commerce (1st year, 2nd year, 3rd year) and Post Graduate also including B.Ed. and M.Ed.

In order to pass the Bachelor Degree examination a candidate must obtain the following minimum marks :

(a) ***Pass Course:***

(i) Minimum in each Paper : 36%
(ii) Aggregate marks : 35%

(b) ***Honours Course***:

(i) Minimum each paper : 36%

(ii) Aggregate Marks : 40%

Division/Class

(i) ***Pass Course***: Students are awarded divisions on the basis of their aggregate marks in all the subjects taken together as follows:

Simple Pass / III Class: 35% marks or more but less than 45%.

First Class: 60% marks or more.

(ii) ***Honours Course:*** The Honours students are awarded division or class on the basis of the aggregate of marks of all paper in Honours subject/group including the papers taken in the subject/ group in the first year. The percentage of marks to get the class is as follows :

Third Class : 40% marks but less than 50%.

Second Class : 50% marks but less than 60%.

First Class : 60% marks and above.

In the Master Degree programmes also annual examination is conducted by the university at the end of each of the academic years which is called Previous and Final covering 50% of the total number of courses prescribed for the whole programme by the Academic Council. A student must attend a minimum of 75% of the lectures, tutorials, seminars, etc. organised by the department during the year to be eligible to appear at the examination.

In order to qualify for Master Degree, a candidate must secure 35% marks in aggregate. Class is awarded on the basis of the aggregate marks obtained in all the papers. Those who secured 45% and above but less than 60% are placed in the First Class.

Scheme of Evaluation in B.Ed.

(1) Practical work and practice teaching is evaluated separately by a Board of Examiners appointed by the University. The Board of Examiners hold a viva-voce test and review the practical work done by each candidate and award one of the following grades to

it. The Board of Examiners also observe at least one teaching class taken by each candidate and award one of the following grades to practice teaching :

Grade O : Outstanding

Grade A : Good

Grade B : Average

Grade C : Failed

The two grades are then combined by the Board of Examiners and a final grade awarded.

(2) Every candidate is examined in theory courses, sessional work, and practical work including practice teaching. He/She shall have to meet the minimum requirements for passing the examination in the manner prescribed.

Technical Education

In 1979, the Arunachal Pradesh Government submitted a proposal for setting up an Institute of Science and Technology, with multiple input and terminality facility. This proposal was accepted in principle by the North-Eastern Council in 1981. At the behest of North-Eastern Council, the Indian institute of Management, Ahmedabad submitted an initial project report in 1982.

The same year, planning commission approved the proposal. However, the Education Ministry called for detailed report and action plan for evaluation. For this purpose, a working group was constituted by North Eastern Council in 1982. The Working Group Report and Action Plan was placed before Education Ministry in September, 1983.

In May, 1984, Planning Commission suggested scaling down of the project in view of the Arunachal University located in the same place.

In June, 1984, an inter-ministerial meeting was held to consider scaling down or retention of the proposed project including provision of degree courses. The consensus was for retention of the project including degree programme For awarding its own degree, it was agreed that NERIST will be conferred university status by an Act of Parliament.

The institute started its academic programme with the admission of students through an Entrance Examination in August, 1986.

General Information - NERIST

North Eastern Regional Institute of Science and Technology (NERIST) was endeavoring, in the past years of its existence, to be a leading institute of learning in the field of applied science and engineering not only in the north eastern region but in whole of India. In its short existence of six years it is persuing the policy of educating the whole man. At the institute both technical and social science subjects are emphasised in order to prepare students to perform equally well as educationists, scientists, leaders in industry, trained engineers and technicians.

The academic programme in engineering and technology at NERIST has been designed to consist of three successive two year bearing modules after matriculation. The three modules are called certificate, diploma and degree. In applied science, a two year Base module and a 4 year Degree module is being offered. Each module provides terminality corresponding to an occupational level, and at the same time provides entry to the next higher module, finally leading to a degree in engineering or technology about six years after matriculation. It, thus, provides vertical and lateral linkages between different occupational levels. The system also allows lateral entry from outside with necessary pre-requisite, at the base of each level.

The institute is a new experiment in the field of scientific and technical education in the country. The structure is a close approach to the current thinking in education policy for vocationalisation at the 10+2 level for reducing pressure at the degree level, at the same time, providing components of the scientific and technical manpower for improving their quality and qualification after some years of work experience. This will also help a meaningful industry-education linkage in the area of secondary occupations. Presently the institute is affiliated to North-Eastern Hill University (NEHU), but it is a step arrangement and in due course it is expected to become a deemed university and award its degree. However, certificates and diplomas awarded by NERIST is recognised by Govt. of India.

The Institute has two faculties—Applied Science and Engineering and Technology.

Course Structure and Syllabi

The course structure and syllabi at NERIST for certificate, Diploma and Degree Modules have been prepared by the faculty of the institute keeping the approved policies in mind and after consulting various available sources materials.

The prime emphasis of NERIST programme is on vocations, especially at the certificate level and to lesser extent at the diploma level. The syllabi of Degree module of NERIST have been kept at par with those of the leading institutions of the country.

At the certificate level, the NERIST programme is prepared to be close to the vocational training offered in 2 years ITI programme and Vocational course by various ICAR Institutes. At the same time, additional training in basic sciences and preparatory course in engineering are imparted keeping vertical mobility of students in view.

The diploma programme of NERIST has been prepared keeping in view the requirements stipulated in the TITI's model syllabi for a 3 years diploma in engineering. The programme at NERIST includes more courses in basic science and interdisciplinary fields spread over four years after matriculation.

At the degree level, the courses have been designed to be at par with the degrees of reputed institutions. Various bridge courses have been designed depending upon the deficiency expected in various groups joining laterally at higher modules. The bridge courses may require an extended period of stay at the campus. These courses have been identified in the course structure.

The certificate and diploma of NERIST have already been recognised by the Minsitry of Human Resource Development, Govt. of India and a notification in this regard has been issued. The degree programme of NERIST has been recognised by the North Eastern Hill University, Shillong. NERIST has been affiliated to NEHU for the award of Degrees.

Eligibility of Admission

The seats at the Base-module (certificate) in NERIST are filled through a competitive examination called NERIST Entrance Examination. The eligibility is as under:

(a) Students who are bonafied residents of the seven sister states. Arunachal Pradesh, Assam, Manipur, Meghalaya, Mizoram, Nagaland and Tripura are eligible. The sons and daughters of Govt. and Semi-Govt. employees working in these states are also eligible for admission.

(b) One should have passed matric or class X examination of 10+2 system, or equivalent with science and mathematics to qualify for admission. Candidates appearing in matric class X examination or equivalent by July 1991 and expecting to pass the same before September 1991 may also appear in NEE-1for consideration for provisional admission.

(c) **Reservation :** 10% seats are reserved for each of the seven states. Remaining 305 seats are filled on the basis of overall merit. Reservation for SC/ST only on seats of states quota will broadly be as per policy of each state subject to any restriction on maximum reservation.

(d) **Physical fitness :** It is advised that the applicant get themselves examined by a registered medical practitioner to assure that they are up to the requisite medical standards.

Registration

General : All students are required to register themselves at the counter of the Academic officer before the commencement of each semester. A student will not be allowed to attend classes unless he/she obtains a certificate from the Academic Officer to the effect that he/she has completed the requirements of registration for the institute of departmental core courses.

Conversion Table

The following conversion table of percentage of marks in 5 points grading system of NERIST is applicable only for the purpose of admission and grant of scholarship.

% of Marks	*Equitable GPA 5 point grading*
50	2.65
55	2.96
60	3.24
70	3.82

Number of Students passed the Successive Modules

Discipline	*Base Module*				*Diploma Module*	
	1988	1989	1990	1991	1990	1991
FACULTY OF ENGG. & TECH.						
Civil	29	38	24	17	26	35
Mechanical	19	30	17	27	18	29
Electrical	19	18	18	09	18	14
Electronic	39	38	29	31	39	38
Computer Science	33	35	29	29	32	35
Agricultural Engg.	00	00	00	04	04	04
FACULTY OF APPLIED SCIENCE						
Forestry	08	20	05	02	00	00
Total	147	179	122	119	137	155

Evaluation

The certificate, Diploma and Degree programmes of NERIST are based on the credit system of evaluation. The prominent features of the credit system are : continuous evaluation of the student's performance, the absence of a pass or a fail on an annual basis, and flexibility to allow the students to progress at their own pace depending on ability or convenience, subject to the regulation on credit requirements.

Each course has a certain number of credits which describes its weightage. A better grade with a specific number of grade points is awarded in each course for which a student is registered. A student's performance is measured by the number of credits that he/she has completed satisfactorily and weighted average of the grade points. Grade points average is required to be maintained for satisfactory progress. Also, a minimum number of earned credits should be required in order to qualify.

Every course is co-ordinated by a member of a faculty, called the course co-ordinator. He/She has the full responsibility for conducting the course, co-ordinating the work of the other members of the faculty involved in that course, holding the list and assignments and awarding the grades. In case of any difficulty the student is expected to approach the course co-ordinator for advice and clarification.

Post-Script

Higher education system has important responsibilities to the developing traditional society like Arunachal as a whole as well as to the educational system itself. The aims and objectives of higher education in the state are little bit different than that of the other states. Thus, the higher education model as practiced in other universities can not be transplanted here directly. An alternative model for education is to be developed for the entire north-eastern States, specially Arunachal. The resources and the content from the environment demand a new approach for higher studies and research.

Access system to higher education have had to become more flexible to accommodate the new needs and dynamics ; in so doing they have increasingly converged to take account of the new demands, while at the same time honouring the values of the traditional system. Thus, the access system should be based only on entrance examination in higher education.

The curriculum for higher education should be redesigned in accordance with the modern development as well as the needs and aspiration of the people of the state. The teaching, learning strategies also are to be examined and developed to cope with the content in higher education. Seperate curriculum development cell should be established in the Arunachal University in accordance with the guidance of U.G.C. Faculty development scheme should be introduced for higher education.

With a view to bring the qualitative improvement in higher education, the evaluation system is to be examined. The prevailing scheme of evaluation neither assesses the intellect of the student nor imagination. There is diversity and richness of new methods and approaches for evaluating the students achievement. Thus, the evaluation scheme in higher education should be rehauled thoroughly. Continuous evaluation process should replace traditional examinations.

Research in education is an essential component for developing the system. Research programme should be launched very urgently. People can not think of higher education without research. Educational theories and strategies are developed on the basis of continuous research and practice. Arunachal University is considering the programme through its various committees.

REFERENCES

1. The New Encyclopaedia Britannica - Micropaedia, 1985, Vol.5.p.917.
2. The New Encyclopaedia Britannica - Micropaedia, 1985, Vol.18.p.I.
3. The Arunachal University Act, 1984.
4. Six Annual Reports of the Arunachal University, 1985 - 1991.
5. Biswas. N.B., Education in Arunachal Pradesh ; A Historical Profile, Arunachal Review, Vol. IV No.7, Itanagar, 1992.
6. Silver Jubilee Souvenir, J.N.College, Pasighat, Arunachal Pradesh, 1989.
7. Husen Torsen (Ed.) The International Encyclopaedia of Education, Vol. 4., OXFORD ; Pergamou Press. 1985.
8. Habung Payeng, Economic and Social change in North East, Criterion Publishers, New Delhi, 1988.
9. Census of India, 1961 ; North-East Frontier Agency General Population Tables.
10. Census of India, 1971, Arunachal Pradesh General Report.
11. Census of India, 1981 ; Arunachal Pradesh, Pt. II General Population Table.

V

TEACHER EDUCATION

Historical Background

The present state of Arunachal Pradesh was once a part of Assam and was then called the North-East Frontier Agency (NEFA). With the attainment of independence, there began a new era of educational progress and development especially in the field of Teacher Education in the region. In December 1947, a teacher's training institute was established in Sadiya (now in Assam), which was under the supervision of the then Education Officer Mrs. Indira Miri, and it was she who started the pioneering work in the field of education. The training institute in Sadiya was established so as to encourage the teachers to play a crucial role in the spreading (expansion) of education in the region. The training institute was established for expansion of education in the interior areas especially among the tribals who were cut-off from the rest of the country. The trained teachers from this training institute were set to the interior areas for opening of new schools. Thus, began a new era in the field of teacher education in the region.

In 1952, the training institute at Sadiya was shifted to another place Margherita (now in Assam) because of some natural calamities. The earthquake of 1950 dealt a severe blow to the expansion programme of the education department. Besides, the subsequent floods washed away almost the whole of Sadiya in 1952 with the result that the training institute was shifted to

Margherita. During the First Five Year Plan, the government spent an expenditure of Rs. 40,899 for the training of the teachers and for one demonstration school at Margherita. The Total number of teachers trained at the Teacher's Training Institute, Margherita from 1952 to 1956 was 160.

In the Second Five Year Plan period the Teacher's Training Institute was converted into a Basic Training Institute called "Buniadi Siksha Bhavan". It was shifted to Changlang (in present Arunachal Pradesh) on 19th December, 1957. The total number of teachers trained between 1956-57 and 1960-61 was about 200-100 each in basic training and in Hindi. Besides, inspecting officers and heads of educational institutions are also deputed for training in the Bhavan.

The teacher's training programme of the *Buniadi Siksha Bhavan* is so designed that the teachers are trained up as multipurpose workers in the interior villages. Thus, on completion of training, when they are posted in the interior places, they function not only as teachers, but also as agricultural demonstrators and emergency doctors. Training in social education is a part of the training course in the B.S.B. and the teachers are fully equipped to organise social education activities in the interior villages.

In the B.S.B. the training is imparted with special emphasis on agriculture, cane and bamboo work, social services and development of culture including songs and dances.

Demand and Supply of Teachers

In pursuance of the constitutional obligations and universalisation of elementary education, there is a phenomenal expansion of schooling facilities in Arunachal Pradesh. It has resulted in greater demand for teachers at all levels, but more particularly at the elementary level. The demand of teachers is generated not only due to increase in enrolments and number of schools, but also because of attrition of teachers due to retirement, resignations, death, etc. There has been significant growth in the number of schools and enrolment at elementary and secondary and higher secondary stages in the state.

Tables below show the enrolment at elementary as well as secondary and higher secondary stages of education in Arunachal Pradesh.

Growth of Primary Schools and Enrolment

Year	*No. of primary schools*	*Enrolment*		
		Boys	*Girls*	*Total*
1960-61	129	NA	NA	4201
1965-66	314	NA	NA	10404
1970-71	506	14751	4168	18919
1975-76	633	NA	NA	36344
1980-81	NA	39775	20129	48835
1986(Sept)	1199	52519	35504	88023
1989-90	NA	62007	45126	107133

Source : Basic Statistics, Directorate of Economics and Statistics, 1986, and Directorate of Education, Govt. of Arunachal Pradesh.

Enrolment of Secondary and Higher Secondary levels of Education

Year	*Secondary level (Class IX & X) Enrolment*			*Higher secondary (Class XI & XII) Enrolment*		
	Total	*Girls*	*% of girls*	*Total*	*Girls*	*% of girls*
1976-77	921	185	20	384	49	13
1981-82	3353	927	28	1626	323	20
1986-87	7452	2239	30	2580	662	25
1988-89	8853	2762	31	3466	856	25

Source : Statistical Books, Arunachal Pradesh, Directorate of Economics, Govt. of Arunachal Pradesh.

Besides the growth in the number of schools and enrolment of students, the state is facing the dearth of trained teachers at all levels of education. The state needs to make more provisions to fulfil the annual requirement of teachers, especially trained teachers at all stages of education.

At present there is one District Institute of Education and Training (DIET) only which admits 100 students for one-year course of elementary teacher education. There is a proposal to open two more DIETs shortly for training of elementary school teachers. In view of shortage of teachers, these DIETs could still continue to offer one-year programme instead of two-years till the demand is met, so that no more untrained teachers are appointed in schools.

Similarly, the admission to B.Ed course under Arunachal University, Doimukh may be increased so as to fulfil the demand of trained graduate and postgraduate teachers. Till 1990, the University admitted 25 students only in B.Ed course to meet the needs of teachers in the state. Estimates of requirement of such teachers may be arrived at by working out present need and future demand.

Position of Teacher Education

Teacher education in Arunachal Pradesh is in its infant stage. There is a backlog of untrained teachers both at primary as well as secondary and higher secondary stages of education. Present position of teacher education in the state is not encouraging. The number of untrained teachers in all the stages outnumbered, the trained teachers as revealed by the following Table.

	Total		Trained	
Year	Male	Female	Male	Female
1985-86	3531	804	1619	302
1986-87	4023	938	1712	331
1987-88	4357	1093	1823	368
1988-89	4794	1180	1883	370
1989-90	5102	1309	2038	381

Thus there is an urgent need for proper and regular in- service as well as pre-service education programmes for untrained Department of education has already started the process of in-service training of its school teachers in the following ways:

(i) Deputation of newly appointed untrained teachers in primary and middle schools to DIET at Changlang

(ii) Organisation of Mass Orientation of school teachers (PROST) programme conducted by the NCERT for the last three years (1986/87 & 1988)

(iii) Teachers from single teacher schools were oriented during 1989 under the operation blackboard scheme

(iv) Some teachers from primary schools are deputed to CCRT, New Delhi for training in puppetry courses.

(v) Organisation of in-service programmes in teaching of Hindi/English for middle and secondary school teachers.

(vi) Deputation of 15 untrained teachers annually from secondary and higher secondary to Department of Education, Arunachal University in B.Ed course since 1988-89.

However, these sporadic efforts will not suffice. A well-planned programme of regular in-service education of teachers need to be developed in the state. Priority should be given to remove the backlog as the proportion of untrained teachers in the state in 1989-90 was about 60 percent which is highest in Arunachal Pradesh at the national level (Ed. Cil, 1990).

Elementary School Teachers

The minimum entry qualification for preparation of elementary school teachers laid down in the document " District Institutes of Education and Training - Guidelines (WHRD, 1989)" is 10+2 or its equivalent. The duration of training is two years. Teachers produced under this scheme will be expected to teach all the subjects in classes I to VIII. It is, however, suggested that such teachers may teach all subjects at the primary stage but only two subjects at the upper stage.

The existing pattern for preparation of elementary school teachers in Arunachal Pradesh is, however, quite different. Students belonging to local tribes are admitted to this training even after Class X. The duration of training is only one year. The minimum entry qualification for not-tribal candidates and those belonging from other states is graduation. This is, of course so out of necessity as the only elementary teacher training institution called *Buniadi Shiksha Bhavan* (B.S.B.) at Changlang is not able to supply the number of trained teachers required in the state.

The B.S.B. which has now been raised to the level of District Institute of Education and Training (DIET), admits 100 students annually but the entry qualification and duration of training have not been upgraded. It is understandable as a short term measure in view of special condition and immediate requirement of teachers in the state. However, in the long run, the state should follow the pattern suggested at the National level for contents and duration of teacher education at this level.

Secondary School Teachers

The other category of teachers is required for teaching different subjects in secondary and higher secondary schools. The minimum entry qualification for preparation of teachers for secondary schools is graduation and for teachers in higher secondary schools it is a Masters Degree in the subject concerned.

The duration of training is one academic year for both types of teachers and B.Ed degree is awarded on its successful completion. These teachers are qualified to teach only those subjects offered by them in their graduation or in their post-graduation (Masters Degree).

In 1988-89, the Arunachal University at Doimukh started the B.Ed degree course and admitted 25 students only to meet the needs of teachers in the state. This number was, however, increased to 35 in 1991-92. But even then, the number is not enough to fulfil the increasing demand of trained teachers in the state.

General Information of Primary Teacher Education Programme

The origin of teacher education in Arunachal Pradesh can be traced back to December 1947 when a training institute for teachers was established at Sadiya (now in Assam) for expansion of education in the interior places of the then North East Frontier Tract (NEFT) which covers the present Arunachal Pradesh and some parts of Assam. The trained teachers from this training institute were sent to the interior areas for opening of new schools. But the earthquake of 1950 and the subsequent floods washed away almost the whole of Sadiya in 1952, with the result that the training institute was shifted to Margherita in Assam. Again on 19th December, 1957, it was shifted to Changlang in Arunachal Pradesh (then NEFA). The training institute was then renamed as the *Buniadi Shiksha Bhavan* (B.S.B.). Now-a-days the B.S.B. has been raised to the level of District Institute of Education and Training (DIET).

Since the establishment of the DIET in Changlang both pre-service as well as in-service teacher training programmes are being imparted in the institute. The DIET was conceived as an institution to bring about educational revolution at the district level with regard to universalisation of elementary education, pre-service and in-service education of educational personnel and non-formal and adult education. But this is the only institute located in the whole of Arunachal Pradesh which imparts training to the primary teachers of the whole state. According to the document, "District Institutes of Education and Training - Guidelines (MHRD, 1989)" the minimum entry qualification for preparation of elementary school teachers is 10+2 or its equivalent. Also the duration of training is two years. But the existing pattern in Arunachal Pradesh is quite different. Students belonging to local tribes are admitted to the institute even after Class X, and the duration of training is only one year. The training institute follows a co-educational system and is managed by the state government.

Objective of the Programme

This teacher training programme should differ from the pre-school one, as the objectives of primary education differ from those of the pre-school education. In view of the increase in the children's maturity and the need for attaining the three main objectives of literacy, numeracy and technocracy, alone with other socio-emotional objectives, special attention will have to be paid to the development of specialised knowledge and skills with regard to content and methodology. However, certain elements of pre-school teacher education, such as psychology of early childhood and play-way methods of teaching, need to be integrated with the primary teacher education programme.

The primary teacher trainee should -

(1) possess competence of the first and the second language, mathematics and in the topics of natural and social sciences related to environmental studies I and II.

(2) develop skills in identifying, selecting and organizing learning experiences for teaching the above subjects in formal and non-formal situations.

(3) possess sufficient theoretical and practical knowledge of health, physical and recreational activities, work experience, art and music and skills for conduction of these activities.

(4) develop understanding of the psychological principles underlying the growth and development of the child of the age-group 6+ to 4+.

(5) acquire theoretical and practical knowledge about childhood education, including integrated teaching.

(6) develop understanding of major learning principles which help in promoting cognitive, psychomotor and attitudinal learnings.

(7) understand the role of the home, the peer group and the community in shaping the personality of the child, and help develop an amicable home-school relationship for mutual benefit.

(8) conduct simple action research.

(9) understand the role of the school and of the teacher in changing the society.

Besides the DIET, there is a State Institute of Education (SIE) in Changlang which offers short-term training programmes to teachers in various subjects. The duration of these orientation programmes on various subjects ranges from 4 days to one month's time. Sometimes these orientation programmes are being assisted by the CIEFL, Hyderabad. The role of the SIE is crucial for teacher education in the state. Its major function being improvement of quality of school education, assumes a special significance for teacher education also. Some of the important functions of the SIE are as under:

(i) It imparts courses of different duration for in-service training of both untrained and trained teachers of the state;

(ii) Acting as a Resource and Learning Centre for academic activities at the state level;

(iii) Organisation of in-service programmes for secondary school teachers, heads of institutions, supervisors, teacher educators and other educational personnel;

(iv) Organisation of meetings, conferences, seminars, lectures, etc.;

(v) Development of instructional packages on curricular areas and additional new topics useful for the schools and teacher education institutions; and

(vi) Assistance to National level institutions like NIEPA, NCERT, in the implementation of certain programmes.

Composition of Students

Though the state government has established pre-service and in-service teacher's training courses, only a limited number of candidates in Arunachal Pradesh seeks admission to these courses. The District Institute of Education and Training admits 100 students in an academic year, but generally it is observed that the actual enrolment in the institute is comparatively very less. In the academic year (1990-91) the total strength accounted to only 25, out of which 19 were male trainees and 6 were female trainees.

The trainees in the DIET are deputed by the Directorate of Education, Government of Arunachal Pradesh. Generally pre-service trainees are deputed to this institution before they are practically posted/assigned the job of teaching in schools. As stated earlier, the minimum entry qualification in this institution is matriculation, and it was revealed in the study that in the present academic session 1990-91, all the 25 candidates are Class tenth passed.

Number of Trainees

Year/Session	*No. of candidates admitted*	*No. of candidates dropped/withdrew*
1985-86	54	5
1986-87	58	1
1987-88	73	4
1988-89	77	4
1989-90	78	9
1990-91	25	-

Staff Composition

The staff employed in the District Institute of Education and Training, Changlang are appointed by the State Education Department. The present composition of the staff in the DIET are one Principal, a Vice-Principal, 7 instructors and 10 office personnels. Out of seven instructors in the DIET, five are male instructors and the remaining two are female instructors. The minimum qualification prescribed for an instructor is graduation in Science, Arts or Commerce with B.Ed or B.T. degree as his/her additional qualification.

In the State Institute of Education, the composition of staff members include a Principal, an assistant Principal, 4 subject specialists and some office personnels.

Curriculum and Syllabus

The District Institute of Education and Training adopts the curriculum framed by the NCERT. The institutional curriculum includes theory papers, practical work, and some co-curricular activities. The theory course include the following papers :

- (i) Course I : Teacher and Education in Emerging Indian Society
- (ii) Course II : Child Psychology
- (iii) Course III: School Organization and Management

(iv) Course IV: Content-cum-methodology of Teaching English

(v) Course V : Hindi

(vi) Course VI: Content-cum-methodology of Teaching Mathematics

(vii) Course VII: Environmental Studies- General Science and Social Science

In addition to these courses, the trainees are suppose to prepare the final lesson plans in English, Hindi, Mathematics and Environmental Studies. Also they are to take part in activities like art work and community work experience, health and physical education, and socially useful productive work. Each of these activities and the theory courses are assigned different marks. All the theory papers consist of 150 marks each, out of which 100 marks are assigned externally and 50 marks internally. The minimum pass marks for each paper is 40 marks. The table indicates the number of marks allotted to each paper.

The institution has a demonstration school attached to it where the trainees conduct their practice teaching. Practice teaching programme is spread in the middle of the session as well as towards the end of the year when the trainees conduct their final teaching practice. Besides, the institution have their own workshop and demonstration farms. The trainees carry out their practical work in the workshop as well as in demonstration farms. Internal assessments are allotted to each trainee on the basis of his/her performance in the demonstration or agricultural farms and various crafts related activities like cane, bamboo, wood works, etc. Also painting and drawing, knitting and embroidery, dancing, singing and modelling, etc. are other practical works that the trainees have to conduct in the institution.

The teacher's training programme of the DIET is so designed that the teachers are trained up as multi-purpose workers in the interior villages. Thus, on completion of training, when they are posted in the interior places, they function not only as teachers, but also as agricultural demonstrators and sometimes as emergency doctors. Training in social education is a part of the training course in the DIET and the teachers are fully equipped to organise social education activities in the interior villages.

Number of Marks Allotted To Each Paper

Sl. No.	*Title of paper (courses)*	*No. of marks allotted to*		*Min. Pass Mark*
		Internal Assessment	*External Assessment*	*(in %)*
1.	Teacher & Education in Emerging Indian Society	50	100	40
2.	Child Psychology	50	100	40
3.	School Organization and Management	50	100	40
4.	English	50	100	40
5.	Hindi	50	100	40
6.	Mathematics	50	100	40
7.	Environmental Studies, General Science and Social Science	50	100	40
8.	Health and Physical Education	150	-	40
9.	Art work and Community work experience	150	-	40
10.	S.U.P.W.	150	-	40
11.	Final lesson Plans in English, Hindi, Maths and Env. Science	-	100	40

Evaluation Procedure

Examinations are held monthly to test the progress of the trainees. On the basis of their performances each month the internal marks are also allotted to the trainees. The final examination is conducted at the end of the session. The final examination is conducted by the Directorate of Education of Arunachal Pradesh.

The results of the institution beginning from 1985-86 to 1989-90 are shown in the table on page 109:

The institution follows various teaching methods such as lecture method, tutorial method, discussions, seminars, field trips, question and answer method, etc. Tutorials and group discussions are frequently adopted for teaching in the institution. For instructional purpose various teaching aids are generally made use of. Some of the teaching aids used in the instructional purpose are television, radio, pictures, maps and slides.

The Result of the Institution For
The Period 1985-86 to 1989-90

Year/Session	*No.of candidates joined the instt.*	*No.of candidates appeared*	*No.of candidates passed*	*No.of candidates dropped*
1985-86	54	49	36	5
1986-87	58	57	20	1
1987-88	73	69	53	4
1988-89	77	73	46	4
1989-90	78	69	64	9

Short Term Teacher Education Programme

The State Institute of Education imparts short-term training programme to the teachers working in secondary schools of the state. It also imparts in-service training programmes for the supervisors, teacher educators, heads of institutions and other educational personnels of the state on short-term basis. It acts as a Resource and Learning Centre for academic activities at the state level. The institution have so far organised various orientation programmes for teachers in English, Hindi, Life Science, Mathematics and Social Science. These programmes are generally of short-duration. Besides subject-specialists, sometimes the instructions are given by experts invited from other parts of the country especially from CIEFL, Hyderabad.

The following table gives an account of some training programmes carried out by the S.I.E. since 1986.

Account of Some Training Programmes Carried Out By the S.I.E since 1986

Year	*Name of Programme*	*Durations (in days)*	*No. of Participants*
1986	Orientation Course for Non-Hindi Speaking Teachers	20	17
	Orientation Course for Course Director and Resource Persons	10	30
	Resource Persons Training	05	33
1987	Orientation Programme for Sec. School teachers in Physics and Chemistry	04	15
	Orientation Programme in Life Sc. & Maths.	04	27
	Orientation Programme in History & Geography	04	24
	Training of Teachers in Teaching of English under assisted by CIEFL	11	52
1988	Orientation Programme for Hindi Teachers	21	26
	Training of Teachers in Teaching English under Assistance by CIEFL		
1989	Training of Teachers in Teaching English under assisted by CIEFL Hyderabad	10	12

Building and Equipments

The District Institute of Education and Training in Changlang covers an area of about 8 acres. The area is devoted to administrative and institutional buildings, play ground, hostels, agricultural farm, demonstration school and teacher's quarters.

Both the administrative and institutional building is located in the same area. There are separate rooms for the Principal, instructors, office, stores, library, classrooms, craft, science and Art rooms.

Just adjacent to the administrative block there is a demonstration school where the trainees conduct their teaching practices. There is a separate common room for both the teachers and students. Also there is a provision for library for both the students and staff members of the DIET. Separate hostel accommodation is made for both male and female trainees. The total strength of students residing in hostels are 60 for male trainees and 40 for female trainees. Generally, 2 to 4 trainees share a room. Both the hostels are located only a few metres away from the administrative block.

To the left of the DIET, the State Institute of Education is situated. The institute covers an area of about 2 acres. The institutional building includes a room each for the Principal, the Assistant Principal, Staff room, office and a lecture room for conducting short-term programmes in the State Institute.

Teacher Education Programme

In 1988-89, the Arunachal University started the B.Ed degree course for both in-service as well as pre-service candidates. In the beginning it admitted 16 students only to meet the needs of teachers in the state. This number was, however, increased to 25 in 1989-90 and subsequently in 1991-92 it was again raised to 35. The course is of one-year duration. The Government of Arunachal Pradesh deputes 15 in-service teachers in each academic year to this course. The rest of the seats are meant for pre-service aspirants. In addition to B.Ed course, the University has introduced M.Ed course since 1989-90 for extending the research and professional upliftment of the teachers in the state.

Objectives of the Programme

(i) To develop in teachers an understanding of the subjects they will have to teach, the objectives of teaching the same and the methods of techniques best suited to teach them;

(ii) To help to familiarise them with the role of the teachers in the emerging Indian society in general, and the North-

Eastern Region in particular, in the background of the various educational problems;

(iii) To help them to observe, analyse and understand the different aspects of pupil development and behaviour;

(iv) To help them to acquire a desired level of skill in planning and organising teaching and learning activities; and

(v) To help them acquire the necessary ability to plan, organise and lead various school activities.

Eligibility for Admission

Every candidate seeking admission to the examination for the Degree of Bachelor of Education shall satisfy the following conditions:

(i) He/she must possess at least a Bachelor's degree (Pass/ Honours) of this University or have passed an examination recognized as equivalent thereto ; and

(ii) He/she must have, after passing the above degree examination, pursued the regular course of study for not less than one academic year attending at least three-fourths of the lectures delivered and satisfactorily completing all the required practical work and at least 20 practice lessons in each of the special teaching subjects in the prescribed manner.

Enrolment

Arunachal University which started the programme of B.Ed in 1988-89, enrolled only 16 candidates in the beginning. Out of these, 14 candidates were in-service and 2 were pre-service candidates. The in-service candidates are generally deputed on seniority basis by the Directorate of Education, Government of Arunachal Pradesh. The following table indicates the total strength, number of deputed and pre-service candidates and sex-wise distribution of trainees since the inception of B.Ed programme in 1988:

Enrolment of students

Session/ year	*Total*	*In-service*	*Pre-service*	*Male*	*Fem*	*SC/ST Male*	*SC/ST Fem.*	*General Male*	*General Fem.*
1988-89	16	14	02	13	03	12	01	01	02
1989-90	23	14	09	15	08	12	02	03	06
1990-91	22	12	10	17	05	14	-	03	05
1991-92	35	15	20						

Curriculum and the Course of Study

A. *Theory*

	Paper	*Written Exam.*	*Sessional work*	*Total Marks*
1.	Teacher & Society	80	20	100
2.	Educational Psychology	80	20	100
3.	Educational Technology	80	20	100
4.	Problems of Education in India with special reference to North-Eastern Region	80	20	100
5&6.	Special courses (any two)*	40	10	50
		40	10	50
7&8.	Teaching Specialization (Any Two)	80	20	100
		80	20	100

Special courses will include:

(i) Adult and Non-Formal Education
(ii) Education and Rural Development
(iii) Special Education for the Gifted and the Backward
(iv) Educational Guidance and Counselling
(v) Educational Management
(vi) Population Education

Teaching Specialization Courses will include:

(i) History
(ii) Geography
(iii) English/Hindi
(iv) Mathematics
(v) Life Sciences
(vi) Physical Sciences

Written examination of courses carrying 80 marks will be of 3 hours duration and those carrying 40 marks of 2 hours duration- to be conducted by the University. Sessional work will be assessed internally by the Department.

B. ***Practical work and Practice Teaching***

This section of work shall consist of two parts, viz., the practical assignment and practice teaching as outlined below :

(1) Practical Work: Every student shall be required to complete one item of work from the list of suggested works in addition to the prescribed exercises in Educational Statistics and submit his/her work book for evaluation.

Section I : **Educational Statistics**

1. Numerical data and frequency distribution
2. Graphical representation of data-Frequency polygon and histogram
3. Measures of Central tendency—mean, median and mode
4. Measures of variability—range, quartile deviation
5. Correlation by Rand—different method

Section II : **Item of Practical Work Assignment**

(Any one item of work to be taken by each student)

1. Construction of an achievement test
2. Administration of a test and interpretation of the results
3. Socio-metic study of a class
4. Development of a programme learning material of about 25 frames
5. Review of a book (title should be suggested by the teacher)
6. Remedial teaching in any school subject
7. Planning and conducting co-curricular activity and presenting a report—Quiz, debate, magazine editing, etc.
8. Case Study of a student/educational programme

(2) Practice Teaching: A minimum of 20 lessons in each of the two teaching specializations shall be given by every student.

Scheme of Evaluation

(1) Practical work and practice teaching shall be evaluated separately by a Board of Examiners appointed by the University. The Board of Examiners shall hold a viva-voce test and review the practical work done by each candidate and award one of the following grades to it. The Board of Examiners shall also observe at least one teaching class taken by each candidate and award one of the following grades to practice teaching :

Grade O	:	Outstanding
Grade A	:	Good
Grade B	:	Average
Grade C	:	Failed

The two grades will then be combined by the Board of Examiners and a final grade awarded.

(2) Every candidate shall be examined in theory courses, Sessional work, and practical work including practice teaching. He/she will have to meet the minimum requirements for passing the examination in the manner prescribed.

Requirements for passing the B.Ed examination and classification of pass candidates

(a) A candidate should get a minimum of 35% marks in each paper both in the written examination and in the sessional part separately with a minimum of 40% marks in the aggregate in the combined marks of the written examination and the sessional work. In Practical work, a candidate should get a minimum of 'B' grade in the combined grade on practical assignment and the practice teaching.

(b) Those who satisfy the minimum pass requirements in written and sessional parts but fail to obtain the minimum aggregate in the combined marks of written and sessional parts may reappear in one course or more courses twice within a period of three years from the date of admission, to the B.Ed course.

(c) Those who obtain the minimum aggregate in the combined marks of written and sessional parts but fail to obtain the minimum in the written part in any one course in the first chance may appear only in that course in the next two consecutive chances to clear that course.

(d) Those who fail to clear the sessional, practical assignment and practice teaching parts may repeat in the part or parts in which failed only once again within a period of three years from the date of admission to the B.Ed course. However, candidates have to clear the sessional, practical parts before they appear for theory written examination.

(e) Written examination marks and sessional marks in each course will be shown separately and also as total in that course.

(f) For the sake of classification of successful candidates the marks obtained in the written examination and the sessional works will be combined and the aggregate of the same will be used. Candidates who obtain 40% and above but less than 50% in the aggregate will be declared to have simply passed. Those who secure 50% and above in the aggregate but less than 60% will be declared to have passed in the Second Division. Those who secure 60% and above will be placed in the first division. There will be no class/ division indicated in the case of practical assignment and practice teaching but the grades obtained will be shown.

(g) Sessional marks in the different courses and the grade in practical assignment will be submitted to the University before the commencement of the theory examination.

(h) Practice teaching will be assessed by an external Board of Examiners appointed by the University and the Chairman of the Board will forward the grades awarded to the University.

Master of Education (M.Ed) Programme

In 1989-90, the Arunachal University started the M.Ed degree course for both in-service as well as pre-service candidates. The course is offered with a view to prepare the educational administrator, educational planners and experts. The programme is launched to keep pace with the New Education Policy, 1986. The DIETs are in need of professional personnel and academicians for running their pedagogical courses as well as for its innovative programmes. M.Ed programme of the Arunachal University will be immense helpful in that direction. In the beginning only two tribal and two non-tribal students were enrolled in the course. Out of the four candidates one was dropped-out. In the second session, i.e. 1990-91 two tribal and three non-tribal students were enrolled. While in the session 1991-92, five tribals and one non-tribal candidates are enrolled.

Eligibility for Admission

Every candidate seeking admission to the examination for the degree of Master of Education (M.Ed) shall satisfy the following conditions:

(i) He/she after graduation must have passed the B.Ed or an equivalent examination from any University in India or an equivalent institution recognized for that purpose.

(ii) He/she must have, after passing the above degree examination, pursued the regular course of study for not less than one academic year attending at least three-fourths of the lectures delivered and satisfactorily completing all the required course work and dissertation as laid down in the relevant Ordinances and Regulations.

Curriculum and Course of Study

The course consists of three core papers (EC : 1, EC : 2, EC: 3) and two optional papers. One of the Optional papers (EC : 4) will be selected from the Optional Group 'A' and the other optional paper (EC : 5) from the optional Group 'B'. The dissertation work is compulsory for all students. The marks in each core and Optional Papers (EC : 1 to EC : 5) shall be one hundred out of which 20 marks are kept for sessional work. The dissertation carries 100 marks. The detailed course structure along with the marks weightage is given below:

Course No.	*Paper*	*Written*	*Sessional*	*Total Marks*
EC : 1	Philosophy and Sociology of Education	80	20	100
EC : 2	Advanced Educational Psychology	80	20	100
EC : 3	Methodology of Research in Education	80	20	100
EC : 4	Option I (Any one paper out of Group A)	80	20	100
EC : 5	Option II (any one paper from Group B)	80	20	100
	Dessertation			100

Optional Group 'A'

1. Educational Technology
2. Early Childhood Education
3. Population Education
4. History of Education
5. Education of Children with Special Needs
6. Educational measurement and Evaluation
7. Non-Formal and Adult Education
8. Curriculum Development and Evaluation
9. Programmes in Teacher Education

Optional Group 'B'

1. Distance Education
2. Guidance and Counselling
3. Environmental Education
4. Comparative Education
5. Education of Tribal Children
6. Advanced Educational Statistics
7. Education for Rural Development
8. Educational Planning and Finance
9. Trends and Issues in Teacher Education

Requirements for passing the M.Ed Examination

(a) The examination for the degree of Master of Education shall be held once in a year at such time and date as the University may decide.

(b) Every candidate shall be examined in theory courses, sessional work, and dissertation for passing the examination in the manner prescribed.

(c) A candidate should get a minimum of 35% marks in each paper both in the written examination and in the sessional work separately with minimum of 40% marks in the aggregate in the combined marks of the written examination and the sessional work.

(d) Those who satisfy the minimum pass requirements in written examination and sessional work but fail to obtain the minimum aggregate in the combined marks of written examination and sessional works may reappear in one course or more courses twice within a period of three years from the date of admission to the M.Ed course.

(e) Those who obtain the minimum aggregate in the combined marks of written examination and sessional work but fail to obtain the minimum in the written part in any one course in the first chance may appear only in that course in the next two consecutive examinations to clear that course.

(f) Those who fail to clear the sessional work may repeat in part or parts in which failed only once within a period of three years from the date of admission to the M.Ed course. However, candidates have to clear the sessional work before they appear for theory written examination.

(g) Written examination marks and sessional marks in each course will be shown separately and also as total in that course.

(h) For the sake of classification of successful candidates the marks obtained in the written examination and the sessional works will be combined and the aggregate of the same will be used. Candidates who obtain 40% and above but less than 50% in the aggregate will be declared to have simply passed. Those who secure

50% and above in the aggregate but less than 60% will be declared to have passed in the Second Division. Those who secure 60% and above will be placed in the First Division.

(i) Dissertation for the M.Ed Examination shall ordinarily be submitted within 90 days from the date of the completion of the M.Ed theory examination. In special cases the Dean, Faculty of Education on the recommendations of the Supervisor may extend the date of the submission of the dissertation for a period of upto 90 days failing which his/her result shall not be declared. Candidates who do not submit their dissertation within 90 days shall not be ranked. To pass in dissertation the candidate must secure 40% or above in dissertation.

(j) Sessional marks in the different courses will be submitted to the University at least two weeks before the commencement of the theory examinations.

Though the state government has established pre-service and in-service teacher's training courses, only a limited number of candidates in Arunachal Pradesh seek admission to these courses. The District Institute of Education and Training admits 100 students in an academic year, but generally it is observed that the actual enrolment in the institute is comparatively very less.

The District Institute of Education and Training adopts the curriculum framed by the NCERT. The institutional curriculum includes theory papers, practical work and some co-curriculum activities. Examinatioins are held monthly to test the prgoress of the trainees. On the basis of their performance each month the internal marks are also allotted to the trainees. The final examination is conducted at the end of the session. The final examination is conduced by the Directorate of Education of Arunachal Pradesh.

The State Institute of Education imparts short-term training programme to the teachers working in Secondary Schools of the state. It also imparts in-service training programmes for the supervisors, teachers educators, heads of institutions and other educational personnels of the state on short-term basis. It acts as a resource and learning centre for academic activities at the state level. The institutions have so far organised various orientation programmes for teachers in English, Hindi and Life Science.

The District Institute of Education and Training in Changlang covers an area of about 8 acres. The area is devoted to administrative and institutional buildings, play ground, hostels, agricultural farm, demonstration school and teachers, quarters. Just adjacent to the administrative block there is a demonstration school where the trainees conduct their teaching practices.

The short-term training programmes organised by the SIE is very limited in number. The survey shows that there is no co-ordination among the programmes run in the institutions. There is no linkage with the University Teacher Education Programme and the programme run by the institutes so far the quality improvement is concerened. Necessary steps have to be taken for the quality improvement. There should be exchange of ideas among the teachers working for the teacher education programme in the state.

VI

ADULT, NON-FORMAL, VOCATIONAL AND TECHNICAL EDUCATION

Spread of literacy has been an important programme since independence, because the Government of India felt that illiteracy is a curse to the individual and to the society. The illiterate lives life of oblivion. In so many ways, his existence is inferior to that of the literate or the educated one. There is little prospect of a reasonable income. It puts obstacles in the way of social and economic progress, economic productivity is materially affected. The illiterate man cannot be profited by the community development programmes. Illiteracy also resists necessary social change.

In a country, which has adopted a socialistic democratic pattern of life and has determined to achieve economic development in the shortest possible, it is very necessary that the entire population should become functionally literate. "Without adult education and adult literacy", says Professor V.K.R.V. Rao, "it is not possible to have that range and speed of economic and social development which we require nor is it possible to have that content or quality or tone to our economic and social development that makes it worth-while in terms of values and welfare. A programme of adult education and adult literacy should therefore take a front place in any programme of social and economic development".

Under these circumstances, on October 2, 1978, a National Adult Education Programme has been launched to liquidate illiteracy in the age group of 15-35. The main objectives of the programme are:

(a) Development of the country's human resources in the vital age group 15-35

(b) Provision of basic literacy skills

(c) Up-grading functional skills

(d) Operating social awareness among the illiterate masses.

The National Policy on Education 1986, envisages that adult education would be a means for reducing economic, social and gender disparities. The principal aim of the new National Programme of Adult Education (NPAE) is to provide education including literacy, to the population in 15-35 age-group, which numbers about 100 millions.

The main features of the implementation strategy will consist of the following (NPE 1986):

(a) Reorganisation of the existing programmes to introduce flexibility and other masses for greater effectiveness.

(b) Application of Science and Technology and pedagogical research for improving the pace and environment of learning.

(c) Establishment linkage between adult education and the developmental programmes

(d) Launching of mass functional literacy programme.

(e) A multi-dimensional programme of continuing education as the instrument for moving towards a learning society.

(f) Creation of dynamic management structures to cope with the targets envisaged.

(g) A distinct slant in favour of women's equality and taking of all measures in pursuance of this resolve.

The planners of the NPE 1986 felt that the past programmes had suffered due to excessive dependence on administrative structures and lack of involvement of the mass organisations, media and the educational institutions. So, it is proposed to correct the imbalance by taking the following measures:

(a) Active cooperation will be sought from political parties and the mass organisations of workers, peasants, women, youth and students.

(b) Effective support will be provided through the mass media.

(c) All developmental departments will be expected to utilise the adult education programme for the furtherance of their objectives.

(d) The entire educational system will commit itself to this cause.

(e) The district, *tehsil* and *thana* level administrative machinery will be involved in NPAE to ensure their support for awareness-oriented adult education programmes.

The National Policy on Education 1986 has emphasised for reorganisation of the existing programmes and many techniques and new programmes have been suggested for improvement of AEP.

Adult Education

With the launching of National Adult Education Programmes in 1978, the Adult Education Programme began in Arunachal Pradesh in 1979-80. In each District, Project Officer (PO) was appointed to look after the functioning of the Adult Education centres. However, the post of Project Officer was upgraded to District Adult Education Officer (DAEO) in 1986. Since then, the number of Adult Education centre have been increasing considerably in all the districts. In order to eradicate illiteracy, the government is also spending a large amount to encourage Adult Education in every part of the State. There are 688 Adult Education centres in Arunachal Pradesh. In the Block levels,

Supervisors have also been appointed to supervise the Adult Education programmes. There are 39 Supervisors in the State and one Instructor is being appointed for each Adult Education centre. In the District, District Adult Education Officer (DAEO) is the head, under the supervision of Deputy Director of Public Instruction of the District.

Districtwise Position of Adult Education Centres— as on 1993-95

Sl. No.	*District*	*No. of AE centres*	*No. of DAEO*	*No. of Supervisors*	*No. of Instructors*
1.	Tawang	29	1	2	29
2.	West Kameng	55	1	4	55
3.	East Kameng	82	1	2	82
4.	Papum Pare	-	-	-	-
5.	L / Subansiri	41	1	6	41
6.	U / Subansiri	85	1	2	85
7.	East Siang	99	1	3	99
8.	West Kameng	103	1	5	103
9.	Dibang Valley	50	1	2	50
10.	Lohit	52	1	7	52
11.	Changlang	54	1	3	54
12.	Tirap	38	1	3	38
	Total	688	11	39	688

Source : A.E. Branch, DPI's Office, Naharlagun.

Every year, Government is spending a large amount of money to run all these Adult Education centres in Arunachal Pradesh. During the session 1993-94, Government has already planned to spend Rs. 70,00,000/- (Rupees seventy lakhs) under Plan and Rs. 42,29,000/- (Rupees forty two lakhs twenty nine thousand) under non-Plan. With this amount, lot of facilities are provided in each centre. Knitting machines, tailoring machines, lamps and kerosene oil, books, pencils, note books, chalks, etc. are provided to the centres for adult learners.

Non-Formal Education

No data is available regarding the number of working children. However, it is assumed that a large number of school children are unable to avail the opportunity of formal schooling because they are to work to supplement family income. In National Policy on Education (NPE) 1986, a new programme of non-formal education has been taken up for these children and for the children of habitations without schools. This programme assumes that NFE can result in provision of education comparable in quality with formal schooling. Modern technological tools - such as solar packs for provision of power in NFE centres, audio-visual aids, radio-cassette player - will be used to improve the learning environment of NFE centres, and learning material of high quality will be developed taking into account the fact that children who work have several assets on which their education should be built.

The non-formal education is envisaged for those children who have never been to schools or have dropped out without completing elementary education. Through non-formal education, out of school children will be helped to come back to schools if they so desired. Those who are not willing to join, they should be helped to develop vocational competency and functional skills. The instructional materials for non-formal education should be flexible, relevant based on local needs.

With a view to fulfill the above mentioned objectives, function of non-formal education system started in Arunachal Pradesh, by the initiation of the Union Government during the session 1984-85 and it continued upto 1985-86 only. Within this two sessions, 72 NPE centres were sanctioned, 22 in 1984-85 and 50 in 1985-86, but only 49 NPE centres were opened and functioned. However, due to paucity of fund, the Union Government postponed to provide fund for continuation of the NPE in Arunachal Pradesh. Since NFE is under the initiation of the Union Government, the Government of Arunachal Pradesh did not take any initiative for its continuation. As a result, all the NFE centres in the State remained defunct from 1986 to 1992 (as per the report given by the State Resource Centre (SRC) Cell, DPI's Office, Naharlagun).

Non-formal Education Centres in Arunachal Pradesh

Sl. No.	*District*	*No. of centres sanctioned* 1984-85	1985-86	*Total*	*Name of Centres functioned*
1.	W / Kameng	2	3	5	Nyukmedung Lish Thrizino Senge
2.	Tawang	2	2	4	Jang Seru
3.	E / Kameng	2	2	4	Chayangtajo Sepra Darlong Dikhalmukh
4.	L / Subasir	2	5	7	Old Ziro Kimin (Papum Pare)
5	U / Subansir	2	5	7	Daporijo Taliha Necho Sujum Dumporijo Muri-Mugli
6.	East Siang	2	7	9	Oyan Muriline Pasighat Ruksin Nari Yiingkiong Boleng Pangin Mebo Balek
7.	W / Siang	2	6	8	Along Town Kaying Pobdi Kabu Derka Kombo Angu Yaki-Tato
8.	Dibang Valley	2	4	6	Dambuk Chata Bolung Jia
9.	Changlang	2	4	6	Khimiyang Khengku
10.	Lohit	2	6	8	Tezu Lathac
11.	Tirap	2	6	8	Borduria Deonlai Mongua Wakka Longo Noksa
	Total	22	50	72	

Source : SRC Cell, DPI's Office, Naharlagun.

However, during the session 1993-94, the Government has planned to start the NFE in Arunachal Pradesh. In this regard, thc Government of India, Ministry of Human Resource Development has sent a telegraphic message, addressed to Shri Tabom Bam, the then Secretary of Education, Government of Arunachal Pradesh vide their letter No. 20Z.C ENLTTA 0045,000 ENLTTA X 1330 CA 4, NEW DELHI SBPO 26 STE 76 for submission of proposal for revival of NFE system in Arunachal Pradesh.

As such, the Department of Education, Government of Arunachal Pradesh has already taken steps for its revival during the current session. Assistant DPI, SRC Sri C.K. Taikam is the incharge of NFE system in Arunachal Pradesh under the DPI. All the sanctioned and defunct centres are likely to be revived and some more new centres are also likely to be opened.

Community Schools

Alongwith Adult Education centres and Non-Formal Education centres, many community schools have been opened in all districts of Arunachal Pradesh. These community schools are opened in such area where formal educational institutions are very difficult to be established or opened. It may be because of extremely less population in the area. Sometimes, these community schools are established alongwith other institutions wherever necessary. In the community schools, both adult and young people are allowed to attend the programme. In every community school, one instructor is appointed and he is paid an amount of Rs. 1,000/- (Rupees one thousand) as honorarium. Earlier it was Rs. 800/- (Eight hundred). Through community education, whole masses are made aware of the various developmental activities which are going on in the world and in India. In Arunachal Pradesh, there are 266 community education centres in different districts. Number of community schools in different districts are given in the table:

To run these community schools, the Government of Arunachal Pradesh, the Department of Education is spending a large amount every year. During 1993-94, Government has already sanctioned required amount for community education. Rs. 31,75,000/- have been sanctioned for the current session.

Number of Community Schools-Districtwise

Sl. No.	*Name of District*	*No. of Community School*	*No. of instructors*
1.	Tawang	9	9
2.	West Kameng	32	32
3.	East Kameng	25	25
4.	L / Subansiri	49	49
5.	U / Subansiri	24	24
6.	Papum Pare	-	-
7.	West Siang	24	24
8.	East Siang	1	1
9.	Lohit	30	30
10.	Dibang Valley	34	34
11.	Changlang	38	38
12.	Tirap	3	3
	Total	266	266

Source : Statistical Branch, DPI's Office, Naharlagun.

Jana Siksha Nilayam

There are many adult learners who are interested to learn more after completion of their adult education course in the AE centres. But it is very difficult for them to join in the formal system of schooling as they are very busy. For such people, the Government has kept provision for continuation of education. Education Department has established many Jana Siksha Nilayam centres in many parts of the State to enable the adult learners to continue their education after Adult Education Programmes. The Jana Siksha Nilayam centres give knowledge and awareness to the adult learners besides 3 R's, they learnt from AE centres. There are 209 Jana Siksha Nilayam centres in different parts of Arunachal Pradesh and in each centre, one instructor is appointed. The instructors are being paid Rupees three hundred fifty as honorarium pay. Jana Siksha Nilayam centres are under the District Adult Education Officer under the supervision of DDPI of the District. In the table below, the number of Jana Siksha Nilayam centres in various districts are given:

Jana Siksha Nilayam Centres - Districtwise

Sl. No.	*Name of District*	*No. of JSN centres*	*No. of instructors*
1.	Tawang	6	6
2.	East Kameng	12	12
3.	West Kameng	24	24
4.	Papum Pare	-	-
5.	L / Subansiri	29	29
6.	U / Subansiri	14	14
7.	West Siang	25	25
8.	East Siang	13	13
9.	Dibang Valley	7	7
10.	Lohit	39	39
11.	Changlang	31	31
12.	Tirap	10	10
	Total	209	209

Source : Statistical Branch, DPI's Office, Naharlagun.

Vocational and Technical Education

In 1976, the National Council of Educational Research and Training (NCERT) document "Higher Secondary Education and its vocationalization" was presented to the country setting out a model conceptual framework for implementation of vocational education. So, programmes for vocationalization of higher secondary education was initiated in 1976.

Being aware of the importance and need for diversification of secondary education—its vocationalization, the Ministry of Human Resource Development, Government of India and NCERT have initiated many actions and made many proposals. Evaluation studies of vocational programmes in most of the States were conducted to provide the findings to the States for implementation.

In spite of all these efforts, the scheme of vocationalization of education has not yet picked up. There have been many factors responsible for the slow progress, such as absence of a well coordinated management system, unemployability of vocational pass outs, mis-match between demand, supply, reluctance in accepting the concept by the society, absence of proper provisions for professional growth and career advancement for the vocational pass outs etc. Renewed efforts are being made by the Government to accelerate progress. Urgent steps to strengthen the vocational education system are therefore imperative.

However, in Arunachal Pradesh, vocational course have not been introduced earlier. In secondary education curriculum, vocational course could not get its pace. Only, during 1992-93 and 1993-94, vocational courses have been included in four higher secondary schools in Arunachal Pradesh.

In Bomdila Higher Secondary School in West Kameng District, vocational education on 'Horticulture' has been introduced. In Doimukh Higher Secondary School too, this vocational education has been introduced to impart education on orchid or fruit gardening in Arunachal Pradesh. In Basar Higher Secondary School in West Siang District, 'Food Preservation' has been introduced as vocational subject and at Pasighat Higher Secondary School in East Siang District. 'Secretarial Practice' such as Typewriting and Stenography has been introduced as vocational course. In other Higher Secondary Schools, no vocational education has been included in school curriculum.

Technical Education is one of the most significant components of Human Resource Development spectrum with great potential for adding value to products and services and for contributing to the national economy and improving quality of life of the people. However, Arunachal Pradesh is lacking in Technical education in the State. As a result, Arunachal Pradesh depends on other States of India for getting technical education of Arunachal students after class XII examination in various technical courses such as Medical, Engineering, Forest, Fishery, Veterinary, Agriculture etc. Arunachal Pradesh has only one technical institute for Diploma and Degree-North-Eastern Regional Institute of Science and Technology, which is under the control of North Eastern Council (NEC). NERIST which is located at Nirjuli, about 15 Kms away from Itanagar, capital of Arunachal Pradesh, is also not sufficient to impart technical education to our students as seats are distributed among the seven states of North Eastern Region.

However, Arunachal Pradesh has some vocational and technical institutions run by the Government and private management. Industrial Training Institute (ITI) Roing is a famous one which imparts technical education to the under matric students. The following table shows the number and names of the vocational and training institutions in Arunachal Pradesh.

Technical and Vocational Training Institutions under Government and Private

Sl. No	*Name of the Institution*	*No.*	*Govt./Private*
1.	Industrial Training Institute	2	Govt.
2.	NERIST	1	Govt.
3.	State Institute of Education	1	Govt.
4.	District Institute of Educational Training	1	Govt.
5.	Health Training and Research Centre	1	Govt.
6.	Gram Sevak Training Centre	1	Govt.
7.	Farmers Training Centre	1	Govt.
8.	Arunachal Forest School	1	Govt.
9.	School of Veterinary Science and Animal Husbandary	1	Govt.
10.	Donyi-Polo Vocational Institute	1	Private
11.	Donyi-Polo Computer Training Institute	1	Private
12.	Donyi-Polo Music College	1	Private
13.	Sports School	1	Govt.

Conclusion

The aim of the Adult Literacy Centres is not only to eradicate illiteracy but for imparting employment generation training and for improving the skills in various arts and crafts. Successful trainees are given financial assistance for setting up handloom and other small-scale industries. The total enrolment of Adults in various centres of Arunachal Pradesh are about 1487. The reasons for low enrolment in Adult Literacy Centres are that they feel too exhausted to attend the classes in the evening after a day long hard toil in the field, secondly, they feel that they are too old to learn all these things. Moreover, they see very limited functional utility of it, they think that by knowing only how to read and write will not fetch them a governmental job - they would have to continue work in the field as before.

Students are given enormus facilities in Arunachal Pradesh. They are given all hostel facilities and stipends, students of lower classes are given free uniforms mid-day meal or tiffin, mosquito nets, blankets and stipend granted to hostlers. Right from Class I to XII they are given text books free of cost. In spite of so many facilities people do not send their children to schools. The reason for this are:

a. Education had a late start in Arunachal Pradesh. So many people especially of interior villages are yet to realise fully the importance of education.

b. Since most of the people of Arunachal Pradesh are poor, solely dependent on agriculture, they need the help of their children in the field. Hence, do not send their children to schools. Even some of the parents who send their children to school had to withdraw from school after six or seven years. This is because of the reason that most of the villages have schools upto primary or middle school level and after passing out from those schools they are to join higher secondary schools somewhere else.

c. Most of the parents cannot afford to send their children due to economical reasons.

d. Some students discontinue their studies after failing in the examination.

In spite of tremendous developments of formal education in the state, the percentage of dropouts is high, a simultaneously problem-shaped in front of the Government to tackle with the dropouts of the school from Class I to X. It reveals from the records that the percentage of droppers from Class I to V are significantly high in Arunachal Pradesh schools. This was an all India Problem for which the Government of India introduced the scheme of Adult Education Programme. Naturally, Arunachal Pradesh did not lag behind to land with the programme in the state to tackle with the problem of the dropouts through different schemes for Adult Education, namely-

1. Rural Funcational Literacy Programme (RFLP)
2. State Adult Education Programme (SAEP).

It may be mentioned in solace that the programme has gained a momentum and popularity amongst the Adults of Arunachal Pradesh not only to secure jobs but for the consciousness which has been created by the growing percentage of literacy in the state.

Also to promote and support the programme of Adult Education the *Jana Shiksha Nilayam programme* has been introduced under the new Education Policy, 1986 having an objective to provide continuing education programme basically for those new literate and dropout students.

VII
WOMEN EDUCATION

Status of Women among Tribals

Before we talk about the status of women amongst the tribes of Arunachal Pradesh, it will be imperative to know the term 'status'. The term status stands for position, role etc. It signifies the sum total of the various culturally ascribed roles one has to play the rights and duties inherent in a social position. Besides the ascribed status, there is also achieved status, which results from one's personal achievements. The concept of 'status' is used to indicate the ordering of individuals in terms of attributes such as level of education, occupation, income, perception of one's status within the home and in the community, decision making roles, restrictions imposed on one's activities, freedom of one's enjoys and so on.

The people of Arunachal Pradesh belong to heterogeneous groups with varied customs, traditions, culture and language. Despite these variations, all the tribes share similarities in food habit, occupation, observation of taboos and mode of living. The code of conduct are guided by the customs and traditional laws of each group. In spite of all these, the position of women in all the tribal communities are broadly same excepting the Akas in which the Rani occupies the prominent position in the society. Thus, it will not be wrong to draw broadly a single account regarding the position of women for all the tribal communities of Arunachal Pradesh.

The women in the tribal societies of Arunachal Pradesh possess a position of subordination to the menfolk. The environment in the early times was not congenial for peaceful life. The nature of duty or role and the demand of the hour placed the men in a superior position. Due to continuous threats from wild beast, hostilities among rival villages and inter-tribal wars, the physically strong menfolk were to engage in outdoor activities and depending the tribal territories and the womenfolk being physically weak were to confine to the household activities and bringing up of children.

The paramount necessity of survival due to threats from inter-tribal war and peace added by superstitions and the cohesiveness of class, groupism and individual tribalism, compels to enforce a strict social norm in the line of customs, traditions and faiths which bounded individuals and families of the tribal people. Despite these social findings, the women were never been under restrictions in movements or strictly confined inside the four walls of the house as found in the societies. The pathetic and perversive conditions like dowry death, bride burning and child abuse are non-existence and a think of unknown to the tribal women of Arunachal Pradesh, though bride purchase is a common practice in certain sections of the tribes.

Though women's position in Arunachal Pradesh is nevertheless important yet had certain rights and duties in the socio-cultural, economical, political and religious fields. All the tribal communities fall under patriarchal or patrilineal system where position of men is superior. In all the important socio-political matters, it is the decision of the men that prevails upon the women. The women have the sole responsibilities of cooking meal, preparing rice beer, collecting firewood, child rearing and other household activities.

Marriages are generally arranged after protracted negotiations in which the consent of the boy and girl are taken into account. In most of the tribal groups like Gallongs, Mishmis, Nishis, etc., bride price were prevalent and accepted, though the quantum differs from community to community and the prices were accepted in terms of kinds or Mithuns. The criterion of selecting a good wife is seen from many angles like the knowledge and abilities of traditional work culture like cooking, brewing rice beer, weaving and other aspects like generosity, chastity and good outer appearance. The girl having all the good qualities were demanded higher as such valued higher price. Poligamy is a common practice in most of the communities and a man can keep as many wives as per his capacities. The girls once married, became the possession of the husband and as such she takes up all the responsibilities of the house.

Divorce is permitted under certain conditions, such as infidelity, barrenness and incompatibility in conjugal relationship. A man can divorce his wife by paying some compensation as fixed by the Village Councils. A woman cannot separate herself from her husband without the consent of the husband. In case of infidelity the husband can divorce his wife without any compensation. A divorced woman can remarry - society does not impose restriction unless social norms are violated. The divorced woman can take the youngest female child in her possession but cannot keep male child who are not infant. In case the child is infant boy, she can keep him but cannot give her own title and return him when grown up. The divorced woman has no right to claim the properties but can take her personal belongings like dresses and utensils.

A widow woman in the tribal communities of Arunachal Pradesh is generally married to the nearest brother of the deceased if available and ready to keep otherwise the chance goes to any one among the nearest clan. In case of issueless widow she has the option to remarry outside the clan if none is available in the in-law's clan or nobody is willing. Generally, outside clan remarriage is not permitted to those widows who have child particularly male child. If such widow forcibly remarries outside the clan, she has to pay due compensation to the in-laws as fixed by the Village Council. A widow is allowed to possess the properties if her husband has but cannot inherit it. She can use it in her life-time if she is not remarried outside the clan but she has no right to dispose of or transfer any of the landed properties. In case a widow remarries outside the clan her right to claim or possess the properties automatically stands cancelled.

In the field of economic activities of the tribal communities, the woman plays a vital role. Most of the agricultural works are done by women except heavy duties like felling trees and ploughing. They look after the pets like poultry, etc. which fetch reasonable income to the family. They also earn supplementary income by doing kitchen gardening and selling the products in the market. During the leisure, they weave cloth for whole family and sells the abundants. Inspite of all these responsibilities, they do not have the property right. A woman cannot inherit the property either of the father or the husband even if she is the lone and immediate survivor of the family. However, they are allowed to keep certain articles like cloths, utensils and to some degree, pets also.

In the socio-cultural fields, the women in the tribal communities of Arunachal Pradesh have their own place. They take active part in the celebration and observation of festivities. They have the sole responsibilities of cooking dishes, preparing wine and its distributions. The offerings to the deities, Gods and Goddesses are performed by the mother of the house. They take active part in the dances with the male members. There are some dances performed exclusively by the unmarried girls of the community.

In the political sphere, participation of women is restricted. In the deliberations and decision making proceedings women are generally excluded. They must follow the decisions and judgments of the menfolk, even if they are having more knowledge and intelligence than their male counterparts.

Thus, it can be concluded by summing up the discussions on the status of women amongst the communities of Arunachal Pradesh that women had no legal status in the past which still continues. She cannot be a member of the traditional Village Council. She has no voice of any consequences in the family affairs. She cannot own and inherit any property, on the contrary, the women are themselves the property of their fathers and husbands.

Position of Women Education

In context of Arunachal Pradesh, not to talk of women education, even male education was a far dream, till 1947, only few boys could attend schools at Sadiya while earning their own rations in a far off place from their own, by doing laborious work. Even after independence, attending schools by girls were a social taboo and only boys had the privilege. The State Government has also not felt the need of opening seperate girls schools, and whatsoever girls schools are functioning in Arunachal Pradesh are run by private entrepreneurs and missionaries. Even though formal system of education has started progressing rapidly in the sixties, women participation in the teaching - learning process was almost nil due to social taboos, negative attitudes of people, lack of awareness and motivation, economic compulsion and above all girls are looked upon as others property.

Male & Female Literacy Percentage of Arunachal Pradesh, 1961-91

Sl.No.	*Year*	*Male*	*Female*	*Total*
1.	1962	12.24	1.42	7.13
2.	1971	17.82	8.71	11.3
3.	1981	27.98	11.03	20.1
4.	1991	51.10	29.39	41.22*

* 32.87% excluding 0-6 years.

Sources :

(a) Census 1961 & 1971

(b) Kadu Marken : A study of growth of Elementary Education in Arunachal Pradesh.

(c) Panda, S. : Changing Profile of Women in Arunachal Pradesh, Echo of Arunachal, Nov. 4, 1992.

Female education in Arunachal Pradesh made its appearance only after sixties. However, starting from almost nil in the sixties, it has made its entry into the literacy map of the State with 3.71 per cent of its women being literate. By 1971 the number of literate women had trippled with a figure of 8.71 per cent of literate women. During the last decade female education has made a tremendous progress in the State. Due to continuous effort of the State Government, changing social situations, growing awareness amongst the female population, there were tremendous effect in the progress of women education in the State. Even though there is virtually no separate girls schools and colleges in the State, co-education is not a deterrent, since mixing up freely of boys and girls is not a social taboo. With every village having a school at present, 90 per cent of girls population in the age-group of 6-14 years are attending schools. At present, every fourth woman in Arunachal Pradesh is literate with a literacy of 32.87 per cent as per 1991 census.

Female Literacy Percentage in Arunachal Pradesh

Sl.No.	Name of District	Total Female Literacy % 1981	1971
1.	Tawang	12.40	2.80
2.	West Kameng		
3.	East Kameng	8.10	
4.	Lower Subansiri	7.6	
			1.65
5.	Upper Subansiri	5.2	
6.	West Siang	13.30	
			4.85
7.	East Siang	15.60	
8.	Dibang Valley	13.50	
			7.37
9.	Lohit District	17.50	
10.	Tirap	9.60	3.47
	Arunachal Pradesh	11.3	3.11

The decade growth rate of 1.42 per cent in 1961 from zero base in 1950s to a growth of 2.6 per cent to 3.11 per cent in 1971 and 2.59 per cent growth in 1981. 11.3 per cent and a growth of 18.09 per cent in 1991 with 29.39 per cent of woman being literate, indicates that the women in the State are making rapid progress in the field of education.

Impact of Education on Status of Women in Tribes of Arunachal Pradesh

The rapid development of education during the eighties has helped to develop a new social order in Arunachal Pradesh. The narrow attitudes and superstitions, groupism and localism have been gradually substituted by scientific approach to problems, togetherness and a common socio-political entity. The impact of expanding education to the younger generations has gradually percolated and effected their elders too. Inter-tribal and inter-caste marriages among the educated generation has established a cordial rapport in between tribes other wise unknown to each other in the past. This has broadened the attitude and outlook of the people and a sense of common feeling and unity in place of historic difference and disunity.

Districtwise Population and Percentage of Literacy

Sl.No.	*District (1991)*	*Population 1991*	*Literacy*	
			1981	*1991*
1.	East Siang	99.985	25.15	35.79
2.	West Siang	89.778	22.25	35.97
3.	Lower Subansiri	1,54,591	18.93	32.74
4.	Upper Subansiri	49,163	12.43	29.70
5.	East Kameng	50,238	NA	30.42
6.	West Kameng	56,402	21.45	36.08
7.	Tawang	27,574		24.88
8.	Tirap	85,210	18.7	24.38
9.	Changtang	92,891		
10.	Dibang Valley	42,928	25.00	37.78
11.	Lohit	1,09,632	27.35	39.55
	Total	8,54,392	20.00	32.87

Sources : 1981 Census.
1991 Census, Manorama Year Book, 1990 & 1992.

In such stage of social and cultural changes among the tribes of Arunachal Pradesh, the fairer sex section are no more a silent and passive spectators. The wind of changes blows through their feet as such a positive attitude towards changes from old social bondages has gradually cropped up in their minds. Various changes in the social, economic and political field has provided greater opportunities and challenges to the educated women. These educated groups women are spearheading the movement against the position of subordination and subjugation in the name of customs and traditions. They no longer recognize the sex as a bar in the social and economic activities. They are demanding more opportunities and equalities in all spheres of life. The age-old ethics of simplicity and loyalty has been taken over by competitiveness and straightforwardness.

Now, the educated women are entering the various professıonals, like lawyer, doctor, engineer, administration and business and other white collar jobs. They are no more content with the single earning of their husband. They favour the concept of economic independents as such, they thought it better to earn themselves. Their perception and value system has been changed. The ethics and materials which mere valued much are worthless. The traditional work culture, dresses and customs are on the verge of extinctions. The traditional dresses are discarded and its place is taken over by Western or latest fashions. The educated wives are no more ready to accept the traditionally ascertained works. Instead of family career, they chose to enhance the family income. Their supported income has enhanced the living standard of the family. It has helped to develop a new tendency among the educated boys to go for educated girls as their life partner.

The arranged marriage system through negotiations is gradually losing its importance among the educated generations. Now love marriage is commonly practiced. Still the greater impact is the choosing of partners among same level of qualification or at least from the educated. A highly educated boy or girl hardly goes back to rural areas and marries illiterate one. Earlier, simplicity, loyalty, work experience, etc. were the criterion of choosing a good bride which is taken over by level of education and income. This tendency of people has further motivated and encouraged the girls to go for higher education for better security in future.

Another recent trend, commonly seen among educated women of Arunachal Pradesh is the positive attitudes towards the small family norms. They have discarded the traditional beliefs that children are gifts of God. The earlier concept of 'larger the family the more the prosperity' has no relevance. The educated mothers give weightage to quality than to quantity of children. The family planning methods are widely accepted by the educated women, this attitude has percolated to the illiterate women of rural areas also. The acceptance of "small family norms" as well as the increasing awareness of "small family is happy family" has encouraged the nucleus family system. No educated daughter-in-law favours joint family to separate on early date. This attitude has eroded the family solidarity and emotional bondage among the family members.

The educated women has identified their rights and duties and their role in the society. Now they are conscious of their socio-economical and political rights. Earlier, they were denied from the decision-making process excepting the Ahha tribe, but now they are openly and actively taking part in the administrative and political activities. Now many women are entering into the State and National level politics and are holding high positions. It has again affected the illiterate women in the rural areas and encouraged to initiate and follow their educated sisters.

The impact of education on the status of women in Arunachal Pradesh is in fact much more and deeper than what has been discussed above. The education has moulded their psychological built up, changed the outlook and attitude and the personality as a whole. Now the level of education is the determining factor of the position of women. The higher the level of qualification, the higher is her social status and the more respects she demand in the community. Rigidity to social customs and tradition, dependency on husband has no more relevance to the educated women.

The impact brought about by modern education, however, has not proved to be an unmixed blessings. The status of women, no doubt, has been improved considerably but at the same time the very social fabrics has been threatened. The tribal ethics of simplicity and solidarity of class has been eroded. The age-old customs and traditions has been tampered in the name of modernisation. The traditional family bondages and norms has been discarded. As a result, family discernity, divorce and unwedded pregnancy has increased among the younger generations. The social values like respect for age and elders, loyalty to class hospitality and simplicity has eroded considerably. These evil effects are but inevitable and universal, for nowhere and never in the history of world, the impact of advancement of evolutionary civilization is in a pure metal but always an alloyed one. What is needed of the hour is slight precaution by the educated and conscious section of the society to preserve the traditional heritage by modifications, as per the need of the time, and thereby minimise the damage on the social and moral values.

Women's Position in Various Communities

A review of the customary status of women in various communities of Arunachal Pradesh is necessary to highlight the contour lines of their position. For convenience of study of the special variations a selected number of tribes from different parts of Arunachal Pradesh has been discussed below :

The *Aka* women, as in most tribal societies, enjoy in reality a better status than possibly women in many sophisticated societies. She is no drudge and keep pace with her husband in most of his economic pursuits. Whatever her legal positions, equal participations remain in the economic sphere in addition to her domestic chores which ensures her position in the family vis-a-vis society.

Among the *Sherdukpen*, the wife does not have any right or claim over immovable property but she can independently rear poultry and even cattle which she can sell on her own, and retain the sale proceeds for her personal use. This ensures her a better personal status and independence in her husband's home.

Among the *Tagin*, the wife acquires a limited right over her husband's property but cannot dispose it of. She can, however, sell the property among the relatives of her deceased husband provided she has no children. Here, again the status is not one of unmitigated subjection.

The *Bagni* custom permits the first wife to have a say in the matter of property inheritance. Daughters are excluded from inheritance but have complete ownership of ornaments such as bead necklaces, and utensils given away to them as dowry in marriage. They are not completely at the mercy of their husbands. The dowry ensures her a real status in marriage.

Among the *Monpas*, daughters have claims to their mother's ornaments. In the absence of sons, daughters have a claim to their father's property. But the next generation, devolution of property reverts to the male line. Nominal bride price with linkage to the social status of the family is existed. Inside family, women enjoy respect and reverence but in public they are not equal to men. Their contribution to the family economy is not less than menfolk. Yet they remain a second rate specia in the male dominated Monpa society.

The Apaiani society has a comparatively better set up for an honourable living for women. Even though society is patriarchal, the women at home enjoy honour and freedom of a rightful participant in family life. Polygamy and plyandry is not formally allowed. Freedom of choice in marriage is allowed.

The Galongs (Branch of Adi) have the unique distinction of practicing a system of fraternal polyandre. Even though the Galong society is well balanced in sex ratio, the system was practiced only due to the burden of heavy bride price on a poor young man and his family members. Monogamy and polygamy also continue side by side, with polyandre. Though the society is male dominated, the women enjoy the privilege of honourable partner at home.

A Padam Minyong (Adi) does not mind looking after a child, and may even lend a hand in cooking while his wife is away from home. The sowing and weeding fall in women's sphere of activities, and are thus an equal partner in joint economic efforts. Though a woman is debarred from the 'Kebang' (Village Council), she has other means of having her voice heard and her influence felt. Beads and ornaments bought by her husband are her property and thus inherited by her daughters and daughters-in-law.

Among the *Mishmis* of Lohit, devolution of property is strictly in the male line. Brothers look after the property if a man dies leaving wife and children. Daughters are entitled to receive their shares in family ornaments, cloths and others, presents at marriage. Among the Idu Mishmis, inheritance is conditional upon the sons performing eschatological rites of their father after death.

A Singpho wife has no right to property, but is free to use it. The widow has a share in the property left behind by her husband.

The Wanchos of Tirap do not acknowledge women's right to

property. Daughters are, however, not totally deprived. They are entitled to get ornaments, clothing, utensils and equipments.

The Noctes, another tribe in Tirap, are patriarchal in all other respects. Daughters, however, are given adequate dowry during their marriage. Women otherwise have free access to their husband's property without, however, any claim on it.

The Tangsa women are permitted to make use of their husband's property, but denied a share of it. Nor can they claim to paternal property, but have free access to it while they live under the parental roof.

The Khampti society is monogamous as a rule with the exception of chiefs and wealthy persons enjoying the privilege of plurality of wives.

From the patterns of actual position of women in Arunachal society as described above, it should be abundantly clear that they are not absolutely left to their fate. The bride price received is balanced, sometimes even unmatched by the amount of dowry given to daughters in marriages. The exchange of gifts by the contracting parties in marriage is an outstanding feature of Arunachal society in general. This endures a better status to women in real situations whatever their legal status theory. One is also struck at once by the aspect of a natural justice which informs the customary laws of Arunachal Pradesh.

VIII
EDUCATIONAL MANAGEMENT

The educational system all over the world is emerging very fast and tremendous changes are taking place. Change in its structure, organisation, content, programmes, objectives etc. are visible. This is the recent year which resulted in the development of a new branch of study known as educational management. It is increasingly becoming important that educational system is to be meaningful. It must have well experienced managerial personnel so as to cope up with the changing content of educational system.

Kendel, while writing the purpose of educational management says that, "Fundamentally, the purpose of educational management is to bring the teachers and the pupil such conditions so as to promote the successful end of education".

The essence of educational management can be seen through its operation and its techniques. Sir Graham Belfour writes very aptly that, "the purpose of educational management is to enable the right pupil to get the right education from the right teachers at a cost within the means of the state so as to enable the pupil to do its best use".

Educational management is a process by which an organisation or institution or an educational enterprise can be managed. It is a process of organising or managing the educational system to achieve the goals of education.

Thus it can be said that while the principles of management is implied in the field of education for managing the educational enterprise with a view to quality output which can cope with the modern scientific advancement within the investment of limited resources is known as educational management.

It is a process by which an organisation or institution or an educational enterprise can be managed. It is a process of organising or managing the educational system to achieve the goals of education.

Educational management can be viewed as a procedure and as a process. It also can be viewed as a specific type of behaviour within the organisation viz., the behaviour of those who carry decisions concerning over-all operations. It is essentially a process i.e. a series of operations for the accomplishment of organisational end. Educational management is a type of behaviour which is subjected to investigation and analysis.

Educational management is not wholly science nor wholly arts. It is both. It is a highly interdisciplinary study. The principles and procedures of educational management has been depicted from the various fields of study like Psychology, Statistics, Economics, Political Science, Physics, etc. Educational management is also a social process.

The nature of educational management is that of a continuous and systematic course of action. Its mode of operation is based on co-ordination and co-operation.

Educational management stand for planning, organising, staffing, directing, co-ordinating, reporting and budgeting.

Educational management refers quality and quantity. Quantity refers to the teaching-learning process i.e. the curricular and co-curricular activities going on in an educational institution and quantity refers to the number of institutions or resources used for. Educational management has its two aspect input and output. Input refers to the physical facilities and the human resources and output refers to the accomplishment of the set objectives or national goals of education.

Thus management is the process of executing the plan and policies for the achievement of the objectives determined by administration.

Schools of Management Theory

Koontz first attempted to classify various managerial approaches and ideas presented at different periods of time into the schools of management theory. His work was advanced by John F.Mee, Joseph A. Litherer, W.W. Cooper E, etc. At present a number of schools of management are being propagated by various authors of books on management. We have used the well established schools of management in the present Arunachal Education system and its management. The management of educational management have been discussed on the above mentioned operative definition of educational management and theory.

Education Management in Arunachal Pradesh

The State follows the system of centralised single line administration where the role of Secretariat is that of co-ordination and overall supervision and the Directorate of Education plays the key role in all academic and administrative matters. Except the technical education, all sectors of education including higher education, art and culture and the libraries are looked after by the State Directorate of Education. The administrative machinery of the State Department of Education consists of the following categories of officials :

Secretariat Level :	
Secretary Education	1
Under Secretary (Education)	1
Directorate Level :	
Director of Public Instruction	1
Joint Director of Public Instruction	4
Deputy Director of Public Instruction	3
Asstt. Director of Public Instruction	6
Accounts Officer	1
Administration Officer	1

State Resource Centre (Adult Education) :	
Deputy Director of Public Instruction	1
Asstt. Director of Public Instruction	1
State Institute of Education (Changlang) :	
Principal	1
Vice- Principal	1
Subject Specialist	6
District Administration :	
Deputy Director of Public Instruction	11
District Adult Education Officer	9
Institutional Administration (General Education) (Gazetted) :	
Principal, Hr. Sec. School	33
Vice-Principal, Hr. Sec. School	39
Head Master, Secondary School	55
Head Master, Sports School	1
District Institute of Educational Training :	
Principal (DIET), Changlang	1
Senior Lecturer	3
Junior Lecturer	11

The Secretary of education exercises the overall charge of the department. There is a State Minister of Education (Chief Minster is currently holding charge of this portfolio) and a Deputy Minister of Education who are directly concerned with policy decisions, planning. The Secretary education is assisted by an under-Secretary and other supporting staff. The function of the education Secretariat are:

i) Policy formulations in relation to education at all levels in the State.
ii) Overall supervision of educational administration, and
iii) Financial and manpower planning.

The policy formulations and financial allocations are directly guided by the Cabinet which holds responsibility to the elected legislative. Observations and opinions of the experts are also sought for policy decisions whereever necessary. Guidelines issued by the Central Government are also followed while making policy decisions.

The State has only one directorate education which is headed by the Director of Public Instruction (DPI). To assist the DPI, there are 4 Joint Directors, 3 Deputy Directors, 6 Assistant Directors, One Accounts Officer and one Administrative Officer. The Director of Public Instruction holds the overall charge of the Directorate and deals with general education with particular references to the following:

1. Deals with all policy matters of education in Arunachal.

2. Directs and supervises all the educational programmes of the State directorate.

3. Supervises and controls the educational institutions financed and managed by the State Directorate.

4. Arranges programmes for the professional growth of teachers.

5. Regulates the working of the State level committees appointed by the Govt. of Arunachal Pradesh.

6. Looks after the appointment, placement, transfer and leave of other officers of the directorate.

7. Selection and deputation of students for education outside Arunachal Pradesh.

8. Creation of posts, continuance and conversion of posts, etc.

The portfolio of Joint Director & Deputy Director of the State are given separately.

The Joint Director of Public Instruction (Planning) is assigned with the responsibility of preparation and finalisation of five year plans and annual plans. Supervision and implementation of all plan schemes, maintenance of plan budget and finalising proposals for opening new schools, inter village schools and up-gradation of middle, secondary, higher secondary schools. The duties assigned to Joint Director (Academic and Science) are matters related to science, education, equipping, maintaining of science laboratories, organising science seminars, exhibitions, affiliation of schools to Central Board of School Education, matters relating to departmental examination, traning and refreshers courses of teachers, administration of DIET and SIE. He is also incharge of UNICEF assisted programmes, population education, national talent search scheme and cultural activities including promotion of art and culture. The Joint Director of Public Instruction (Establishment) is required to attend matters related with the appointment, transfer and posting of gazetted officers, maintaining service books, leave accounts and pension matters, revision of pay scales and keeping the seniority list of all categories of staff.

The assignments of Joint Director (Adult Education and Higher Education) are the following:

(i) Matters connected with appointment, transfer, posting, leave and study leave of lecturers and principals of colleges.

(ii) Grant-in-aid to University.

(iii) Award of Stipends/Scholarship to SC/ST students pursuing studies in and outside the State.

(iv) Selection and admission of students for higher studies and professional courses.

(v) matters relating to College and University education and creation of posts in colleges. He also looks after the national service schemes, national literacy mission and monitoring and evaluation of adult and non-formal education programmes in the State. The Deputy Director of Public Instruction (General) deals with the sanctions of all non-plan schemes, admission of students to Sainik Schools, Rastriya Indian Military College and other approved residential schools and sanction of stipends and scholarships, transfer of students within the State, matters related to mid-day- meal schemes to schools and framing/finalisation of rules for awarding stipend to Scheduled Tribe students of Arunachal Pradesh. Matters relating to All India Educational Survey and Survey of educational administration, teacher education etc. are dealt by the Deputy Dirctor of Public Instruction (survey).

1. Education Minister
2. Education Secretary
3. Under Secretary : Superintendent 1 U.D.C- 2
   Steno 1 L.D.C- 3

		Asstt.	4	Peon - 4
4.	Personal Office :	Steno	1	
		U.D.C	1	
		Driver	1	
		Peon	2	

5. Arunachal Pradesh University
6. Director of Public Instructions
7. Joint Director Public Instructions, Planning Branch
8. J.D.P.I. Higher & Adult Education.
9. J.D.P.I. Academic Science & Maths
10. J.D.P.I. Establishment Branch
11. Principal - SIE
12. D.D.P.I. General Branch
13. Principals : Degree College
14. D.D.P.I. Higher Education
15. D.D.P.I. Science and Maths
16. A.D.P.I. Youth Service
17. A.D.P.I. Adult Education - Monitoring & Ets
18. Principal DIET
19. A.D.P.I. Science & Maths
20. A.D.P.I. Academic & Examination
21. Vice-Principals
22. Account Officer Budget & Acc Branch
23. Administrative Officer
24. A.D.P.I. at present with Operation Black Board
25. Gazetted Cell
26. Confidential Cell
27. Personal Office
28. Subject Specialists - 6
29 Asst. 1
30. Asstt. - 1, U.D.C.- 1, Peon - 2
31. Steno - 1, U.D.C.- 1, Peon - 2
32. Suptd. - 1, Steno.- 1, Asstt.- 2, UDC - 1, LDC - 2, Driver - 1, Peon. - 2
33. Suptd. - 1, Asstt.- 1, UDC - 3, Driver - 1
34. Suptd. - 1, Asstt.- 1, Steno-1, UDC - 4, LDC - 1, Driver -1, Peon- 2

Besides, there are six Assistant Directors of Public Instruction (ADPI) who shall assist the Joint Director and Deputy Directors and also carry out responsibilities assigned independently to them. The six Assistant Directors are specifically meant for (i) Science and Mathematics education (ii) Youth Services (iii) Academic (N) Operation Black Board (v) Adult Education and (vi) Career guidance. The Accounts Officer looks after the budget provisions and expenditure of the directorate, matters relating to audit, maintenance of cash books, bills, CPF accounts and also functions as internal finance officer of the department. The administrative officer is incharge of all matters relating to organising, planning and controlling of the office of the directorate, procurement of vehicles, stationary, accommodation and attandance of the staff.

Administrative Setup at the District and Lower Level

Educational administration at the district level is mainly controlled and directed by the Deputy Directors of Public Instruction (DDPI). To assist him in administration, there is a set of field officers/ staff such as District Adult Education Officer, Asstt. District Education Officer. Adult Education Supervisor and supportive staff DDPI holds overall charge of education at the district and lower levels. He has to exercise the financial powers delegated to him for the drawl and disbursement salary of the district staff and also authorised with inspection/supervision and management of educational activities. Districts Adult Education officer co-ordinates and directs the adult programmes in the district. Assistant Education Officers and Adult Education Supervisors are responsible for maintenance of records, reports and returns in respect of the schools and adult education programmes in the block under their charge. They also assist the DDPI in inspection and supervision. Besides in each block there is an Assistant District Education Officer or Assistant Education Supervisor to co-ordinate the educational activities. Areas in which treasury/banking facilities are available, principals of the Higher Secondary Schools are delegated with financial powers.

School Complex

A scheme of school complex was implemented in the state of Arunachal during the year 1988-89. In this scheme, a number of primary and middle schools are grouped with a secondary/higher secondary school which functions as a lead/pace setting school. The head masters of all the schools under the chairmanship of headmaster of the lead school form a committee to chalk and implement the development and welfare programmes for the schools. For the effective implementation of the scheme a district level committee has also been constituted with District Commissioner as the Chairman and District Education Officer as member Secretary. The major objectives of school complex are :

(i) to provide assistance and co-operate for educational institution at various levels for raising the overall standard of education.

(ii) to bridge the gap between educational institutions at different levels.

(iii) to facilitate decentralisation of supervision, and

(iv) to arrange mutual exchange of materials and man-power for uniform growth of institutions in the school complex.

Although the scheme has been implemented in 1988-89, it has not yet been possible to overall schools in the state under this scheme due to geographical and communication constraints.

Involvement of Local Bodies

In 1967, Panchayati Raj was introduced in the State with 3 tier set up: Gram Panchayat (Village Level) Anchal Samiti (Block Level), Zilla Parishad (Dist. Level). The Anchal Samities are under Sub-Divisional Officers and Zilla Parishads under Deputy Commissioners in their respective areas. Though as per Government instructions, every school is to have a management Committee but such committees do not form part of the Gram Panchayats. Similarly, Anchal Samiti has not separate education committees or any direct involvement in educational administration of the area. The same is the case at the district level. Though these committees do make some suggestions for opening and upgrading of schools for the Education

Department for consideration while finalising its developmental plans. The decision making role of local bodies with respect to establishment of schools needs special mention. The proposals discussed and mooted through the Gram Panchayat are submitted to the respective Anchal Samiti. The Anchal Samitis scrutinize and recommend the proposals to the Zilla Parishad which in turn, may modify and approve the proposals for incorporating in the district plan. This district plan is sent to Government for sanction and making budgetary provisions for final implementation. There are also traditional village Councils in addition to Panchayats but role of both these organisations is minimal in educational administration.

Community Participation

The local community does not have any definite and significant role in the decision making and involvement in the educational programmes. But its role cannot be ignored altogether. The local community initiates the proposals for establishment of schools, implementing schemes through Gram Panchayats. They also provide land, assist in the construction and maintenance of school buildings and also tries to equip the school with minimum requirements. They cater to the needs and extend help to the staff and students to a certain extent and in turn seek advice and consult teachers in matters related to academic aspects. Important community festivals, celebrations and school functions / programmes are organised as joint ventures of students, teachers and members from the local community. The teachers were held with high esteem and respected by the village community. All sorts of co-operation were accorded to him; at times firewood, vegetables, eggs, meat, even rice and other essential commodities supplied to make him a part of the society for the cause of education. It is true still in some areas that the school ration supplied from district headquarters is carried by local people to schools travelling forty or fifty miles, and one of the village elders is elected as school Secretary to co-operate with teachers for mobilising the village folk to spare their wards for learning. Village elders even escorted the children to school, village Kebangs were held to discuss about the school education and unwilling parents were even fined for not sending their children to schools. The concept of newly incepted community schools envisages to extend pre school and elementary education to young tribal boys and girls upto 14 years of age and adult and non-formal education to adults and youths unable to attend to schools.

Non-Government Agencies in Education

Non-Government educational institutions run by voluntary organisation have also contributed significantly for the progress of education in Arunachal Pradesh. There are only five voluntary organisations which sponsors educational institutions in the State which are Vivekananda Kendra Shikasha Prasar Vibhag (13 schools), Rama Krishna Mission (2 schools), Rama Krishna Sarada Mission (1 school), Boum Kakir Mission (2 schools) and Doni-Polo Mission (2 schools). The above mentioned voluntary organisations are autonomous, guided by their own recruitment policy and service regulations. The Mission schools follow the syllabus and prepare students for the CBSE examinations. These schools receive grant in aid from the Government. While dealing with the educational institutions run by voluntary organisation, it may be mentioned that there does not exist any private aided or un-aided schools in Arunachal.

The non-Governmental educational institutions run by the voluntary organisations receiving grant-in-aid in Arunachal Pradesh are the R.K.Mission Schools at Along; twelve Vivekananda Kendriya Vidyalayas and two schools each run by Doni-Polo Mission and Bom KaKir Mission. It may however, be pointed out that all schools run by voluntary organisations do not receive grant-in-aid from the Govt. of Arunachal Pradesh. For instance, Doni-Polo Vidya Bhavan at Itanagar run by Doni Polo Mission has its own financial source and endownent.

Grant-in-Aid Policy for Non-Government and Voluntary Organisation

The rules for grant-in-aid to the voluntary organisations functioning in Arunachal Pradesh are governed by Govt. vide order No. ED (G) 3/35/84 dated Itanagar 25 January, 1986. It recognised a non-official voluntary organisation constituted administered and maintained by collective private enterprise with the aim of advancement of social or economical welfare of cultural activities of a particular section of people of community of the area as a whole. Application for grant-in-aid to an educational institution run by a voluntary organisation in Arunachal Pradesh may be entertained by the Director of Public Instruction on whose recommendations the Govt. may consider sanction of the scheme and financial assistance. Such educational institutions to become eligible for grant-in-aid must possess undisputed land of their own or the land allotted by the Government of Arunachal Pradesh for construction of educational buildings. Besides, the schools run by the voluntary organisation also must be affiliated to any recognised Board of Secondary Education in India recognised by the State Department of Education. The amount of grant-in-aid may be recurring and non-recurring which are to be decided by the Secretary (Education) in consultation with Secretary (Finance) Arunachal Pradesh. In case the non-recurring grant-in-aid exceeds Rs. 10000 or recurring grant-in-aid exceeds Rs. 25000 per annum, approval of the competent authority is necessary. Besides, the celling limit of grant-in-aid to any voluntary educational organisation by the Govt. is not to exceed 80% of the expenditure involved for the implementation of any scheme during a year both in case of renewal and in respect of new case for grant-in-aid. However, in special case, the above celling limit may be enhanced to 90% and even 100% by the concerned authorities in consultation with the Finance Department for those institutions which are established in difficult for slum areas of the State.

Financial Management

The Director of Public Instruction being the head of the Department, is solely assigned with all the financial powers. Under the D.P.I., there are 37 drawing and Disbursing Officers operating at the district level, institutional level and area level throughout States. The budgetary provision is made in respect of elementary education, Secondary education, higher education (University and College), adult education, Sports and Youth Services, text books, laboratory equipments, Stipend, grant-in-aid, teacher's training, functional and residential buildings. Besides, the State Government follows the rules and regulations of Central Government and continues to follow the pay scales and other allowances of Central Government to its employees. Regarding the administrative structure in financial aspects, the accounts officer represents the finance department and works under the direct functional control of the DPI at the directorate level. The accounts officer delegates and guides all the matters relating to financial management of the department. The other drawing and disbursing officers at the district, institutional and area level discharge duties as per the laid down procedures and practices for budget formulation and functions in direct co-ordination and cohesion with the Director of Public Instruction. With regard to budget formulation, the drawing and disbursing officers estimate and submit the requirements of the budgeted funds against the given plan period in respect of their representative jurisdictions to the Director of Public Instruction. While submitting the budget estimates, the drawing and disbursing officers under education department, like their other counterparts, split the financial requirement under two heads of plan and non-plan. At the directorate level, the estimates of the budgeted fund requirements submitted by all the drawing and disbusring officers of the department are compiled and consolidated by the Director of Public Instruction in respect of the whole education sector vide the following heads of accounts:

I. The Major head - General Education

II. The Minor heads -

(a) Elementary education

(b) Secondary Education

(c) Text books

(d) Other Expenditure

(e) Stipend

(f) Grant-in-aid

(g) University and Higher Education

(h) Teacher's Traning

(i) Adult Education

(j) General and

III. The Major head - Sports and Youth Services

Direction and Administration

In accordance with the existing practice of procedure, the Director of Public Instructions submits the plan budget based on the Annual Operating Plan, (A.O.P) with supportive documents to the Finance Department through the Secretary Education for budget allocation. The plan budget is considered by the State Planning Board based on the plan allocation from the Central Government. Besides, the budgetary provision exists in the form of centrally sponsored schemes and the North Eastern Council Schemes on cent percent assistance. The non-plan budget is constituted by the requirements of the committed expenditure, its preparation necessitates to work out the estimate of actual expenditure under the heads mentioned above. Accordingly the estimate of committed expenditure is also under various heads submitted by all the drawing and disbursing officers for their respective jurisdictions to the Director of Public Instructions who in turn compiles, consolidates and submits the same to finance department. After having obtained the endorsement, the Secretary Education forecast budget estimates. The submission of forecast budget estimate is performed twice during the year, first time during the month of September and the next in January. After the fund is alloted, the Director of Public Instructions, Govt. of Arunachal Pradesh sends sanction communication to the drawing and disbursing officers and signals to go ahead with the task of planned programmes.

The practice of auditing the budget account is done annually. The auditors from the Accountant General visits and formally audits the accounts of the Departments. Besides, there exists the provision for internal auditing. The internal auditing of accounts of education departments like others is conducted by the auditors from the office of the Director of Account under the Department of Finance, Govt. of Arunachal Pradesh. While auditing the accounts, the auditors are summoned to point out irregularities and guide the drawing and disbursing officers to maintain the same as required. In course of auditing, if any irregularity is pointed out, the drawing and disbursing officers are obliged to meet up the queries probed by the auditors. So far, the audit of accounts of the voluntary organisation receiving grant-in-aid from the Government of Arunachal Pradesh, the principal executive of the organisation in question, gets the accounts audited by chartered accountant and submit the same to the Government.

Educational Planning

The present system of educational planning in Arunachal Pradesh is highly centralised and does not cater to long term and medium term plans. Educational planning forms a part of the overall State Planning process and involves planning functionaries from State Planning Board, State Secretariat and Directorate of Education. It may be mentioned that there is a planning cell at the Directorate headed by one of the Joint Directors of Public Instruction. At the district level, the Deputy Directors of Education (DDPI) are responsible for educational planning. In preparation of the plan proposals, the sectoral approach is followed. Financial allocations are made in respect of primary, secondary and higher education (inclusive of University Education). It also considers science education, technical education, scouts and guides, games and sports, non-formal education, adult education etc. The planning also makes provision for incentive schemes such as awards of scholarships, student stipend, freeships and merit scholarships. It also caters to the needs of training and refreshers courses for teachers and extends grants-in-aid to institution run by the voluntary organisations. They also take into consideration the centrally sponsored schemes and the priority of plan proposals. The education Directorate prepares plan as per the guidelines received from the State Department of Planning and Development and submits the same to Secretary (education) for administrative scrutiny and onward endorsement to the State Planning Board for approval. Whatsoever system of planning exists, is centralised where as decentralisation is limited to breaking down the target for the lower levels to achieve. From the above, however, it may not be counted that the field officers have not been granted freedom of action. In day to day working, the different agencies, particularly the district functionaries are adequately independent. They do have their own official machinery, statutory powers and the personnel of the department in the districts are exclusively under the control of the districts heads of the department. These district heads exercise even transfer and posting of staff within their jurisdiction of district. It has to be mentioned here that if anything goes wrong, the matter is referred to the Director of Public Instruction for redressal or immediate appropriate action.

Development of Collegiate Education

It was in 1964, for the first time, that the Jawaharlal Nehru Government College, affiliated to the Guwahati University in the neighbouring State of Assam, was established at Pasighat to impart under-graduate education. The Second Government College was set up. It was set up in 1979 at Itanagar. Due to continued agitation and turmoil and consequent disruption of studies in Assam, affiliation of these colleges had to be transferred to the Punjab University in 1980. Two more Government Colleges, were started at Tezu and Bomdila in 1986 and 1988 respectively.

The Arunachal University

The Arunachal University was set up on April 1, 1985 in persuance of the Arunachal University Act., 1984. The object of the University is to disseminate and advance knowledge by providing instructional and research facility in such branches of learning as it may deem fit and endeavour through research, education, training and extension to play a positive role in the Socio-economic and cultural development of Arunachal Pradesh based on the rich cultural heritage of its people. During the short span, the University has grown into a premier, affiliating, teaching and research institution imparting higher education in the state. The University is located atop Rono Hills near Doimukh, 25 kilometers away from Itanagar on a site of 302 acres adjacent to the river Dikrong surrounded by perrenial forests. The beautiful natural scenery and the quiet serene atmosphere afford an avenue for academic growth and excellence. The jurisdiction of the University extends to the entire State of Arunachal Pradesh and has at present four colleges affiliated to its imparting instruction in faculties of arts, science and commerce. The University for the first time in 1986 conducted examinations for students of the affiliated colleges on the basis of syllabi and courses of study of the Punjab University. The Arunachal University has since framed its own courses of study for both the under-graduate and post-graduate programmes and conducts examination accordingly. The University offered Master Degree Programmes in History, Political Science, English, Economics and Education (B.Ed and M.Ed.) during the session 1991-92. Arrangements have been made to establish the Department of Geography and a Centre for Tribal Research. The University library is housed in a spacious module of the main administrative building. It has over 15,000 books and subscribes to more than 100 Indian and Foreign journals. A separate section has been set up for books and materials on Arunachal and North-East with a view to develop research perspectives on folk literature, culture, customs and traditions of the people in this region. As per the University Act, the President of India is visitor of the University and the Governor of the State its Chancellor; and the University bodies of Executive Council, Academic Council, Planning Board, Finance Committee, Faculties and Board of Studies have been constituted. The Arunachal University is member of the Association of Indian Universities and Commonwealth Universities. The University is receiving the financial assistance from the State Government and steps have been taken to obtain the UGC recognition for financial grant to the University.

Teachers in the University as well as those in the colleges are recruited by open selection on an all India basis with qualifications prescribed by UGC. They are given the UGC scales of pay in addition to DA at the Central Govt. rates, special compensatory allowance as admissible under Govt. of Arunachal Pradesh rules and semi furnished free quarters for residence.

Post-Script

Arunachal Pradesh, situated in North-East India, is an underdeveloped strategically important land with a rich cultural heritage. It became a constituent state of India in 1987. It is a sparsely located thinly populated, tribal territory with gorgeous mountains and perennial forests. The economy of the state is primarily agrarian and traditional Jhum cultivation is practised extensively. There is hardly any major industry in the state. The area is inhabitated by a number of tribes and sub-tribes with different dialects and distinct socio-cultural characteristics.

The educationally and economically backward region appeared on the educational map of India at the dawn of independence figuring only three primary schools. The progress of education was rather slow till 1960. The state also figured the lowest literacy rate at the national level, the percentage being 11 and 20 percent in 1971 and 1981 respectively. However, the state witnessed significant achievement in the development of education during the last two decades. The Government has given emphasis on universalisation of primary education through cent percent enrolment of all children of school going age and prevention of dropping out as well as eradication of illiteracy from the group of 15-35 years. The medium of instruction is English and the schools are affiliated to Central Board of School Education. There is a remarkable increase in the enrolment, efforts have been made to spread education in remote far flung villages and 62 community schools have been set up with a view to provide pre-primary, primary, adult and non-formal education programmes in small village habitations with active participation and direct involvement of the community. The state has a multi-faculty teaching cum affiliating university having facilities for post-graduate teaching and research. The University has four colleges affiliated to it offering 3 year degree courses (pass as well as honours) in Arts, Science and Commerce following the 10 + 2 + 3 pattern of national education.

Keeping in view of the tasks and challenges ahead there is a need for reform in the system of planning and management in education. The educational activities should be linked with the planned programmes of development and welfare schemes for the people of the state. A State Advisory Board of Education may be constituted for integrating all the activities concerned with human resource development. It should be represented by renowned educationists, planners, scientists and members of public life, women and youth forums and voluntary organization. Community should be directly and actively associated with the planning and implementation of education programmes in all sectors of education and District Board of Education can be assigned with the co-ordination and monitoring of all educational programmes including that of adult and non-formal education. At the state level at least three directorates should be created, one for school education, another for higher and technical education and third one for adult and non-formal education including art and culture. This is found essential as the areas of higher education and technical education remain relatively neglected and special attention should be made to promote functional literacy in the state by strengthening the non-formal education programmes. The directorate can also look after the preservation of culture and traditions; the art forms, libraries, museum etc. and also co-ordinate the sports and youth welfare and programmes of Nehru Yuvak Kendras and other voluntary bodies. A State Council of Educational Research and Training (SCERT) should be established as an autonomous organization to lay down broad guidelines and decide priorities of various academic and Teacher education programmes and to continuously review programmes of SIE, SRC, DIETS and adult and non-formal education agencies.

Educational and vocational guidance and counselling services are not offered to students of Arunachal. The state should take immediate steps to have a guidance bureau, and centres should be set up in educational institutions for providing career informations and counselling services in personal and professional problems of student community. A State Board of Secondary Education can also be set up which should undertake the responsibility of evolving curriculum, preparation of text books and study materials, and conduct of the examination in the schools. It is recommended to evolve a decentralised system of educational planning and administration with a multi-level framework at the institutional district and state levels. Micro level plans may be prepared for achieving universal primary education and eradication of illiteracy. The state has initiated the experiment of having school complexes. It is suggested that the system of school complexes should be adopted as an integral part of administrative set up and not merely as an experiment in isolation.

The school complex should become the lowest unit of area planning and management for all institutions upto elementary level.

The state has to follow a multifaceted approach for the promotion of functional literacy. Significant achievement has been observed through the programmes in enhancing the literacy level to 32.1 percent in 1991 from a mere 3 percent in 1961. Although the main focus of the adult education should be on 15-35 age group, there is enough justification to encourage the spread of literacy in the 35+ age group also. The state should adopt three distinct approach for the success of this programme i.e. centre based approach, volunteer based approach and campaign approach. The programmes of adult education need to be backed by a strong system of continuing education.

REFERENCES

1. Elwin, Verrier, A Philosophy for NEFA, Itanagar Directorate of Research, Government of Arunachal Pradesh, 1988 pp. 190 - 201.
2. Furer - Haimendraf, C Change and Development among Tribes of Arunachal Pradesh, Tribes of India, Delhi Oxford University Press, 1989. pp 286 - 312.
3. Haldipur, Krishna. Around the Hills and Dales of Arunachal, Shillong: North-Eastern Hill University, 1985
4. Machenzie, A. The North-East Frontier of India, Delhi : Mittal Publications, 1989.
5. Mibang, T. Social Movements in Arunachal : A Search for answer, News star, Guwahati 16 Sept, 1991, pp 3-4.
6. Mohanta, B. Administrative Development of Arunachal Pradesh 1875-1975, New Delhi : Uppal Publishing House, 1984
7. NIEPA, Educational Administration in Arunachal Pradesh (A survey Report), New Delhi : National Institute of Educational Planning and Administration, 1980.
8. Sharma, H.C. Statistical Handbook of Arunachal Pradesh 1989, Shillong : Directorate of Economics and Statistics. Govt. of Arunachal Pradesh. 1990.
9. Singh, Emergence of Arunachal Pradesh as a state, Delhi : Mittal Publications, 1989.
10. Yadav,G.C. Educational Scene in Arunachal. Arunachal Newsletter, August 15, 1991. p 7.

IX

PANCHAYATI RAJ AND EDUCATIONAL PLANNING

Prospects and Problems

The winning of independence has not worked any miraculous change in the people of the country as a whole. The traits inherited from colonial times constitute inhibitions and obstacles to development which leads to contributes to a large percentage of the world's illiterate population. Whereas Gandhiji hoped that complete restructuring of the Indian educational system would ensure that service to the poor acquired a priority exceeding all other national concern. After forty years of experimenting with education Gandhiji came to the conclusion that the Panchayats could be very effective for the upliftment of the village and the development of village industries of national importance should be in the hands of education and that too on educational lines. So, he laid down, "Every panchayat will be expected to attend to the education of boys and girls in its village.' Nehru also opine that the progress of our country is bound up with the progress of our villages. If our villages make progress, India will become a strong nation. Therefore, we decided that in every village there should be an institution—village Panchayat with more powers. And the important institution which we need in our villages is the school. Every village should have a school so that villagers should be able to receive education. And women should get equal opportunities for education.

Inspite of that the people of the country are not merely insufficiently educated ; they are being miseducated on a huge scale. Of course, the government is conscious of the gravity of the problem and moving ahead with new vision of institutional planning and implementation.

Since independence, India has been making efforts in institution building for the development of the country. If the national development has any meaning in the context of education, it has to be first and most important to institutional planning from the grass root level through democratic process. In order to generate more enthusiasm and evoke more participation of the people in the process rural reconstruction and development than hitherto received, the institutional device was thought proper. This institutional arrangement is known as 'Panchayat Raj'. It is an innovation in the field of institution building. Many would like to call it as an experiment in institution building in the rural sector. The late Pandit Jawaharlal Nehru opine that introduction of Panchayati Raj is a revolutionary and historical step. It was the outcome of national consensus. The development of education is an essential element in this Panchayati Raj Institution. Because education interacts and is interdependent with the process of institutional development. Social structures, policies, and goals exerts their influence on the education sectors, as on other sectors, while the education sector influences economic and social development by systematic application of scientific knowledge. Thus, it has become impossible to talk of development without bringing in the subject of education. Education does not jump, it is a gradual process of great subtlety which is linked up with the local social and political institution. In the present chapter, the author on the above background has attempted to analyse the important role and function of Panchayati Raj institution in developing the school education in three sections. The first section deals with the basic concept of Panchayati Raj which is followed by the analysis of the Panchayati Raj in Arunachal Pradesh and its role in education. The third or the last section deals with prospect of school education through Panchayati Raj alongwith the possible problems and measures to over come those problems.

Panchayati Raj—A Philosophy for Democratic Decentralisation

The philosophy of development that emerged in India after independence emphasised the involvement of the numbers of the national community into a web of relationships and institutions that would enable them to actively participate in the process of decision making affecting their welfare and progress. The move to diffuse power to grass root bodies was first initiated in 1952 through the programme of community development projects. Since then the participation of the people in the rural development process has become the cornerstone of Panchayati Raj system in India which was introduced in 1959 on the recommendation of the Balwant Rai Mehta Committee. Of course, the whole concept of Panchayati Raj was evolved on the Gandhian principle. As Gandhi believed that democracy should be rooted in the villages. "My idea of village Swaraj is that it is a complete republic .... The Government of the village will be conducted by the Panchayat of five persons, annually elected by the adult villagers, male and female, possessing minimum prescribed qualifications. This will have all the authority and jurisdiction required .... The Panchayat will be the legislature, judiciary and executive combined to operate for its year of office .... Here there is perfect democracy based upon individual freedom." Thus, it reveals that the genesis of the philosophy of Panchayat was laid in Gandhi's thought in which the village was made the centre of planning and the implementation of developmental activities was to be with the masses. The Panchayati Raj system got the shape of a three-tier system of rural local government - Panchayats, Panchayat samities and Zila Parishads (with different nomenclatures in different states).

If we review the whole Panchayati Raj system we will be able to see that various models, thoughts and arguments have been put forward for restructuring and redesigning the institutional process from the Balwant Rai Mehta Committee and the views of various political scientists like Dougles Ensminger, Iqbal Narain, S.N.Dubey, Mukherjee and Bandhyopadhyay etc. to the Constitution Act., 1993.

Whatever may be the structure but the basic philosophy remain the same that Panchayati Raj is a process and that the basic component of the process is the growth of effective and viable institutions. The method of democratic decentralisation is institutional, and the development of the institutions is a process which will have to be encouraged and nurtured. Panchayati Raj institutions, having a vital role in rural development, thus become an apparatus of development administration and an expression of democratic decentralisation of a relatively more radical variety. The author does not like to involve in the discussion of various models of Panchayati Raj nor it is the perview of the present section. He simply wanted to analyse the educational channel in Panchayati Raj within the latest Act and the model introduced through the parliament giving importance to the basic philosophy of Panchayati Raj is the upliftment of villages by the villagers themselves with some assistance from the human, technical, and material resources of the government.

Panchayati Raj and Education in Arunachal Pradesh

Panchayats assume the important instrument of decentralisation at the grass roots level in a vast diverse and complex country like India. India's over 600 million village populace gets the right to rule itself. Panchayati Raj has been at work in various stages for nearly three decades. Arunachal Pradesh introduced Panchayat Raj in 1967 with an elected Agency Council at the apex. As in other parts of India, Arunachal Pradesh also followed the similar structure of Panchayat system - the Gram Panchayat at village level, the Anchal Samiti at Block level, and the Zila Parishad at the district level with the time to time amendment. The objective of Panchayat Raj in Arunachal was explain by NEFA as follows:

"The Panchayat in NEFA will be the prime agency for rural development. It will provide a sound basis for economic and political growth. Secondly it will provide workable medium through which the rural people would be able to express themselves on various problems of the area and also to evolve on integrated community approach for solutions of problems that concern the entire Agency. The Panchayat will not only be a decentralised form of administration, it would be much more than that".

A research study was conducted by Talukdar reveals that the Panchayat perform instrumental functions in regard to their welfare and developmental works and direct functions in regard to their elective role and certain remunerative enterprises under taken by them. Thus, it is seen that as in other parts of India, in Arunachal Pradesh too, the Panchayats are expected to be the prime agency for rural development. The smooth working of democracy in Arunachal Pradesh has shown a stable political process.

The Panchayat have succeeded in bringing about a number of changes in the socio-political spheres and in setting in motion a process of political transition and modernisation at the grass root level in Arunachal Pradesh. The political isolation is broken. The village is now a part of a larger political unit and it has frequent contact with the administration through the Panchayat.

By this time the Central Government had brought out the 72nd Constitutional Amendment and it had become an Act after being duly signed by the Parliament of India on April 24, 1993. It has now become the 73rd Constitutional Amendment Act. It is primarily an enabling enactment for the establishment of Panchayats.

On the enabling plan, the amendment requires the states to (a) establish at the very base a Gram Sabha comprising all eligible voters in the village to which the Panchayat will be accountable. (b) mandatory periodic elections every five years and where superseded in mid-term election within six months and (c) reservation to ensure representation of women in Panchayats. In accordance with the amendment Arunachal Pradesh Panchayat Raj Ordinance was passed on 18th April, 1994[2]. Panchayat election was conducted in Arunachal Pradesh. Popular participation in the Panchayat in Arunachal is very encouraging. The Panchayat system is promoting the consciousness among the life of the people in the state. It is helping the people to direct participation in the process of all round development in the villages. At present, there are 2012 Gram Panchayats, 79 Anchal Samitis, 11 Zila Parishads in the state.

There are 3257 habitations in the state out of which 1778 are having primary schools and 1479 habitations are without primary schools, out of 1478 habitations 1150 habitations are below 100 population slab and 110 are 200 or more population slab where primary schools or I—V. are opened during 1989-90 since there are 1150 habitations below 100 population slab without facility for primary education situated in the remote interior areas where it is not feasible to open primary school with hardly 10 children available for primary education. On experimental basis one community school has been taken in one of such locations with provision of a regular teacher for providing formal school education to the children and also non-formal education and adult education. Remarkable progress has been achieved in the field of education. The census report 1991 reveals that there are 858, 392 population in the state. The literacy rate is 32.87 (male 41.34% and female 23.03%). There are 284 pre-primary schools, 1144 primary schools, about 230 middle schools, 73 secondary schools, 48 higher secondary schools, 4 colleges and a University. Thus, it reveals that now Arunachal Pradesh possesses 1823 educational institutions with the total enrolment of more than 161,000 students and more than 6,000 teaching staff.

At present there are 571 centres of Adult education with an enrolment of 30,392 functioning under RFLP. There are 72 non-formal Educational Centres functioning in various places.

Democratic decentralisation through Panchayats as a means to usher in a new social order for the socio-economic transformation of the rural community of Arunachal Pradesh has been accepted by the Government of Arunachal Pradesh. The 73rd Amendment has given a Constitutional status. The legislature has the power to decide what functions to transfer to the panchayats and what not. The Government of Arunachal Pradesh has decided to delegate the power and functions of panchayats through the Arunachal Pradesh Panchayat Raj Ordinance, promulgated 18th April, 1994[3]. So far the education is concerned this ordinance confer the functions of Gram Panchayat in the following:

1. Promotion of public awareness and participation in primary and secondary education.
2. Ensure full enrolment and attendance in primary schools.
3. Promotion of Adult literacy.

While the Ordinance has stated the functions of Anchal Samiti with regard to education is in the following:

i. Promotion of Primary and Secondary Education.
ii. Construction, repair and maintenance of primary school buildings.
iii. Promotion of social education through youth clubs and Mahila Mandals/Samitis.
iv. Promotions of rural artisan and vocational training.
v. Implementation of Adult literacy.

The Zilla Parishad is the district level Panchayat body constituted for every district. The Schedule III of the ordinance under clause 100 refers the following activities with respect to the education of the district.

1. Promotion of educational activities in district including the establishment and maintenance of primary and secondary schools.
2. Establishment and maintenance of Ashram schools and Orphanages.
3. Survey and evaluation of educational activities.
4. Establishment and maintenance of rural artisan and vocational training centres.
5. Encouraging and assisting rural vocational training centres.
6. Planning and implementation of programmes of Adult Literacy and non-formal Education Programmes.
7. Promotion of educational, economic, social and cultural and other interests of the weaker sections.

Prospects of School Education in Panchayati Raj

It is seen from the preceding section that the Panchayati Raj Ordinance has made it clear that the school education is to be the concern of the village Panchayats, Anchal Samitis and the Zilla Parishads. Now the question is how the management of the school education is to be transferred to the Panchayats. Further, how the academic and technical matters such as curriculum text books, examination system, training of teachers and academic guidance are to be managed by the Panchayats. Whether the budgeted money which is being spent on the management of school education in the rural areas directly by the state department of education be transferred to the respective Panchayat Samitis. All these aspects are to be thoroughly examined and decision should be taken very consciously. If the proper institutional planning is made within the every stage of institution like Village Panchayat or Gram Panchayat, Anchal Samiti and Zilla Parishad then education can make a headway in the state. Before transferring the school education to the Panchayat the following strategy can be developed. In every Gram Panchayat a local Education Committee is to be constituted. Few members from the Gram Panchayat, some of the educated members of the Gram Panchayat and representative from Anchal Samiti will constitute the Committee. And this Committee is to be accountable to the Gram Panchayat as well as to the Anchal Samiti with respect to the management of the schools in the villages. Similar type of Committee is to be constituted in the Anchal level and Zilla Parishad level.

Primary Education is the foundation upon which the rest of the education system is built. Experiences and treatment received at the primary stage can have a profound effect on a child's future attitudes and achievements. Thus, the primary education is to be transferred in a phase manner and experimental basis. Local Panchayat Committee is to be oriented of the management of the primary schools. Then we can expect discernible improvement in the working of schools in the hand of the Panchayati Raj in respect of enrolment of students, attendance of teachers as well as students in the schools and effective supervision. Formal appraisal can be made very easily so far the performance of the school. Whereas in a centralised school system it is not possible to do so, particularly in the remote areas where transportation and communication is a great hardle.

Under the management of the Panchayat Committee the villages school will be having autonomy as well as there will be accountability of the teachers. Similarly accountability of the committee members will make them responsible to take interest in the enrolment drives.

The very important impact of Panchayat management may create the feeling of belongingness of the schools to the villagers. Due to proximity of the management of the local body, the teachers are to be regular. The teachers will also have to be the part of the entrepreneur.

The village primary schools which are formally being supervised from the district level will be supervised in a better way from the block level. People's participation for schools building and for arranging equipment for schools will be coming with the same enthusiasm as the local people are building the schools since the introduction of modern education in the state.

Zilla School Board can be constituted for managing the construction of the schools, administration and supervision. Academic Curricular and Co-curricular activities, Finance and Evaluation system of the schools in panchayats also can be managed by Zilla School Board.

Panchayati Raj can easily facilitate and solve the problems of languages in the school education of the state. There are 22 major dialect in the states. All these dialect can be introduced in the area concerned schools. Text books and teaching materials can be prepared in local languages.

Need based curriculum and the course can be developed and implemented easily in the schools. A district education committee of the Zilla Parishad should be set up for the administration of primary education. Not more than half the members of this committee should be members of the Zilla Parishad. The remaining members should be educators or persons interested in education.

There should be an appointment committee at the Zilla Parishad level for the recruitment of teachers. A whole time officer of the status of deputy inspector of schools should act as secretary of the district education committee.

The authority to transfer teachers should be vested in the Secretary at the Zilla Parishad level. As a matter of policy a teacher should not be transferred as far as possible and no transferred should be made within a period of 5 years unless there are special reasons.

In very brief, it can be assumed that if the local community is involved through Panchayati Raj in school education, the enrolment would rise, the rate of dropouts would decrease, the conditions of schools would improve, percentage of literacy would rise, the disparity between the rural urban areas, between male and female, between one district and another would minimise.

Problems of School Education in Panchayati Raj

Transfer of school education to the Panchayati Raj will be a bold experiment. Like every experiment this one also will be facing initial problems of management and human relation. Human mind is by nature conservative and any innovative programme has to face the resistance. If primary school education is transferred to Panchayati Raj all primary school teachers automatically become employees of the Panchayat instead of the state. In India it is considered a great privilege to be a government servant, because of the security of service and other benefits.

Sometimes, the members of the Anchal Samitis and Zilla Parishads may misuse their powers in matters of teachers appointment and transfer, promotion, pupil's examination and evaluation. Corruption may take place in the system through the understanding of the teachers and the members.

Teachers may be used for party politics. The most important problem in Arunachal is the insufficient number of specialized skilled, efficient teachers, teacher educators, educational planners in each district level or Anchal level. Education Committee of local bodies may have suffered from financial and administrative disabilities.

Another bottleneck from which Panchayati Raj may suffer is the existence of too many parallel departments engaged in similar developmental programmes. The existence of parallel organisation make bureaucracy more powerful and reduce the power of elected representative of the community. Panchayati Raj, visualised as an instrument for development in the country side, and for the exercise of local initiative, is a major threat to the power and influence of the urban elite[4].

Conclusion and Remarks

If education in the Panchayati Raj is to make headway, its control will have to be vested in the educated leaders of the community and the technical personnel of the education department. The bureaucrats do not want to loosen their held but ultimately power will have to vested in the elected representatives of the community because they know better where the problem lies. Finally we can say that it is the will of the people for the success or the failure of any institution of Raj. If sincere political and social will is there then only school education through Panchayati Raj can bring out the desired goals of education.

NOTES

1. The NEFA Panchayati Raj Regulation, 1967, remaining in operation for the last 25 years from 1969 to 1994 was amended time to time as follows:

   (a) The NEFA Panchayati Raj (Amendment) Regulation No.4 of 1970.

   (b) The NEFA (Administration) Supplementary Regulation No.4 of 1971.

   (c) The NEFA Panchayati Raj (Amendment) Regulation No.2 of 1972.

   (d) The NEFA Panchayati Raj (Amendment) Act. 1980.

   (e) The NEFA Panchayati Raj (Amendment) Act. 1987.

   (f) The NEFA Panchayati Raj (Amendment) Act. 1992.
2. Arunachal Pradesh is among those states who has ratified 73rd Constitution Amendment Bill. The legislative Assembly of the State on a resolution moved by the Chief Minister, Sri Gagong Apang, ratified the Bill in March, 1993.
3. The Arunachal Pradesh Panchayati Raj Act, 1994 (Bill No. 3 of 1994).
4. The Economic Weekly, October, 7, 1961.

REFERENCES

Dubey, S.N. (1981) : Organisational Analysis of Panchayati Raj in R.B. Jain (Ed), Panchayati Raj.

Indian Institute of Public Administration, New Delhi.

Ensmiger, D.(1981) : Democratic Decentralisation : A new Administrative

Challenge in R.B.Jain (Ed) Panchayati Raj. 11PA, New Delhi.

Gandhi, M.K. Collected works. Vol XLVI P.240.

Mukherjee, N and Bandhyopadhyaya. D (1993) : New Horizon for West Bengal's Panchayats : A report for the Govt. of West Bengal.

Narain, I.(1981) : Democratic Decentralisation : The Idea.

The Image and the Reality in R.B. Jain(Ed), Panchayati Raj, 11PA, New Delhi.

Govt. of Arunachal Pradesh(1994) : Panchayati Raj Ordinance. 1994.

Patil, V.T.(1983) : Studies on Gandhi, Sterling Publishers, New Delhi.

Sharma, M.L. (1987) : Gandhi and Democratic Decentralisation in India. Deep and Deep Publications, New Delhi.

Talukdar, A.C. (1987) : Political Transition in the Grassroot Tribal India, Omsons Publications, New Delhi.

BIBLIOGRAPHY

Allen, B.C., 1905, *Assam District Gazzetters*, Calcutta.

Banerjee, A.C., 1946, *The Eastern Frontiers of British India.*

Barua, B.K., 1969, *A Cultural history of Assam*, Guwahati

Barthakur, J.K.,1971, *Census of India, Series 12*, Arunachal Pradesh, Part-II.

Barkataki, S., 1969, *Tribes of Assam*, New Delhi

Bhattacharjee, J.B., 1989, *Sequences of Development in North East India*, New Delhi.

Bose, Monilal, 1979, *Historical and Constitutional Documents of North-Eastern India*, 1824-1973, Delhi.

Burman, S.C. 1963, *NEFA - The Land and Its People.*

Banks, J.A., 1981, *Multi-ethnic Education*, Boston.

Chakraborty, L.N., 1973 *Glimpses of the Early History of Arunachal*, Shillong.

Chakraborty, A., 1971 *A History of Education in Assam*, Guwahati

Choudhury, J.N.,1983, *Arunachal Pradesh - From Tract to Union Territory*, Delhi.

Choudhury, J.N., 1982 *Arunachal Panorama*, Itanagar.

Dalton, E.T., 1872, *Descriptive Ethnology of Bengal.*

Debi Renu, 1988, *The Progress of Education in Assam* (1882-1973), Delhi.

Das, L., 1989, *Development of Secondary Education in Assam 1874-1947*, Delhi

Elwin Verrier, 1964, *A Philosophy for NEFA*, Shillong

——1968, *Myths of North East Frontier of India*, Shillong

——1965, *Democracy in NEFA*, Shillong.

——1970, *A New Book of Tribal Fiction.*

——1959, *India's North-East Frontier in 19th Century*, OUP, Bombay.

1988, Reprint, *Art of NEFA India*, Itanagar.

Furer-Haimendorf, 1982, *High Landers of Arunachal Pradesh*, Delhi.

Gait, E.W., 1986, *A History of Assam*, Calcutta.

Gopal Krishanan, R., 1994, *Arunachal Pradesh: Land and People*, Delhi.

Haimendorf, C.V.Furer, 1989, *Tribes of India*, OUP Calcutta.

Jha, S.D., 1986, *Arunachal Pradesh- Richland and Poor People*, New Delhi.

——1990, *Socio-Economic Profiles of Arunachal Pradesh*, Delhi.

——1967, *The Wealth of Arunachal Pradesh*, Delhi.

Luthra, P.N., 1971, *Constitutional and Administrative Growth of the North-East Frontier Agency*, Shillong.

1974, *Nagaland - from a District to a State*, Shillong.

Kar, B.C., 1977, *Teacher Education in Assam*, Delhi.

Mackenzie, A. 1884, *History of the Relations of the Government with the Hill Tribes of the North East Frontier of Bengal*, Calcutta.

Mibang, T, 19, *Education in Arunachal*, The Educational Review, Madras.

Raikar, Y.A. and Chatterjee, S., 1981, *Archaeology in Arunachal Pradesh*, Shillong.

Rao, V.V., 1976, *A Century of Tribal Politics in the North* - East, Delhi.

Roy - Burman, B.K, 1970, *Demographic and Socio-Economic Profiles of the Hill Areas of North East*, Delhi.

Rustomji, N.,1955, *Tribal Administration in the NEFA*, Govt of India, The Adivasis.

Rustomji, N., 1973, *Enchanted Frontiers*, OUP, Bombay.

Sarkar, N., 1980, *Buddhism among the Monpas and Sherdukpens*, Shillong.

Sarkar, N.,1981, *Tawang Monastery*, Shillong.

Sukla, B.K., 1959, *The Daflas (Nishi)*, Shillong.

APPENDIX

Educational Institutes: A Glance

Arunachal Pradesh

University	-	1
Engineering Institute	-	1
Polytechnic	-	1
Industrial Training Institute	-	3
Forester Training School	-	1
Farmer's Training Centre	-	1
Horticulture & Forest College	-	1
Colleges	-	7
Higher Secondary Schools	-	68
High Schools	-	103
Middle Schools	-	329
Primary School	-	1280
Pre-Primary Schools	-	137

www.arunachalpradesh.nic.in

Assam

Type	*Nos.*
University	5
IIT	1
Engineering college	3
Medical college	3
General College	226
Junior College	76
Agriculture College	2
Law College	9
Veterinary College	2
Higher Secondary School	599
High School	3915
Middle School	8019
Primary School	31888
Pre-primary school	482
Industrial &Technical school	32
Polytechnic	8

www.databank.nefi.com

Meghalaya

Type	*Nos.*
University	1
General College	45
Teacher Training College	2
Higher Secondary School	40
High School	532
Middle School	1044
Primary School	4685
Industrial &Technical school	7
Polytechnic	1

Nagaland

Type	*Numbers*
University	1
Colleges	40
Higher Secondary School	4
High School	236
Middle School	418
Primary School	1399
Polythchniques	2
Industrial Training Institutes	5

Manipur

Type	*Nos*
Agriculture University	1
Industrial Training Institute	7
Institute	2
Polytechnique	1
University	1

Sikkim: Educational Institutes

Type	*Nos.*
Secondary School	90
Primary School	380

Tripura: Educational Institutes: (2000)

Type	*Numbers*
University	1
College	22
Higher Secondary School	215
High School	392
Middle School	435
Primary School	2068
Pre-primary school	2513
Industrial &Technical school	4
Polytechnic	2

Literacy Rates in North-Easterns States vs. India

State/Union Territory	*1991*			*1997*		
	Person	*Male*	*Female*	*Person*	*Male*	*Female*
1. Arunachal Pradesh	41.59	51.45	29.69	60	69	48
2. Assam	52.89	61.87	43.03	75	82	66
3. Manipur	59.89	71.63	47.60	76	86	66
4. Meghalaya	49.10	53.12	44.85	77	79	74
5. Mizoram	82.27	84.61	78.60	95	96	95
6. Nagaland	61.65	67.62	54.75	84	91	77
7. Triupura	60.44	70.58	49.65	73	79	67
INDIA	52.21	64.13	39.29	62	73	50

Source:(i) Registrar General of India, Decennial Census Reports.
(ii) National Sample Survey Organisation, 53rd Round.

Literacy Rates for SC/ST Population by Sex – 1991 in North-Eastern States

State/Union Territory	*Scheduled Caste*			*Scheduled Tribe*		
	Person	*Male*	*Female*	*Person*	*Male*	*Female*
1. Arunachal Pradesh	57.27	66.25	41.42	34.45	44.00	24.94
2. Assam	53.94	63.88	42.99	49.16	58.93	38.98
3. Manipur	56.44	65.28	47.41	53.63	62.39	44.48
4. Meghalaya	44.27	54.56	31.19	46.71	49.78	43.63
5. Mizoram	77.92	77.54	81.25	82.73	56.67	78.74
6. Nagaland	—	—	—	60.59	66.27	54.51
7. Triupura	56.66	67.25	45.45	40.37	52.88	27.34
INDIA	37.41	49.91	23.76	29.60	40.65	18.19

Source:Registrar General of India, Decennial Census 1991, Series 1 Paper 1 of 1993, Primary Census Abstract for SC and ST Reports.

Total Enrolment in General Education by Level, 1998

(Thousands)

State/Union Territory	School Level				Senior Secondary	Graduate and above	Total
	Pre-Primary	Primary	Middle	Secondary			
1. Arunachal Pradesh	36	150	44	19	7.3	3.7	260
2. Assam	23	3817	1305	549	296	172	6162
3. Manipur	86	237	107	59	10	43	542
4. Meghalaya	145	303	80	31	14	12	585
5. Mizoram	2	134	47	24	4.8	8.3	220
6. Nagaland	85	204	68	27	12	5.9	402
7. Triupura	171	441	128	60	23	15	838
INDIA	2834	108782	39487	17947	9294	5654	183999

Source: Ministry of Human Resource Development , Selected Educational Statistics — 1997-98.

Enrolment of Boys in General Education by Level, 1998

(Thousands)

State/Union Territory	School Level				Senior Secondary	Graduate and abov	Total
	Pre-Primary	Primary	Middle	Secondary			
1. Arunachal Pradesh	20	82	24	11	4.6	2.8	144
2. Assam	13	2025	774	306	186	113	3417
3. Manipur	46	127	58	31	6	22	290
4. Meghalaya	73	152	42	16	8	6.8	298
5. Mizoram	1	71	24	12	2.7	4.7	115
6. Nagaland	47	104	35	14	6.8	3.5	210
7. Triupura	85	240	71	35	14	8.8	454
INDIA	1558	61329	23646	11230	5907	3524	107194

Source: Ministry of Human Resource Development , Selected Educational Statistics — 1997-98.